*Memoirs
and
Opinions*

Memoirs
and
Opinions
1926-1974

Allen Tate

THE SWALLOW PRESS INC.
CHICAGO

Published by
The Swallow Press Incorporated
1139 South Wabash Avenue
Chicago, Illinois 60605

First Edition
First Printing June 1975

This book is printed on recycled paper

LIBRARY OF CONGRESS CATALOG CARD NUMBER: 75-10757
ISBN 0-8040-0662-8

"Stopping by the Woods on a Snowy Evening" by Robert
Frost. From *The Poetry of Robert Frost* edited by Edward
Connery Lathem. Copyright 1923, 1969 by Holt, Rinehart
and Winston, Inc. Copyright 1951 by Robert Frost. Reprinted
by permission of Holt, Rinehart and Winston, Publishers.
"To the Reader" by Charles Baudelaire. From *An Anthol-
ogy of French Poetry from Nerval to Valéry in English
Translation* edited by Angel Flores, Doubleday Anchor
Books. Copyright 1958 by Stanley Kunitz, trans. Reprinted
by permission of Angel Flores.
"To the Reader" by Robert Lowell. Copyright by Robert
Lowell. Reprinted by permission of Farrar, Straus and
Giroux, Publishers.

I am greatly indebted to Morton Weisman and Donna
Ippolito of The Swallow Press for their patience and their
intelligent grasp of the plan of the book.

To Helen

to whom I owe my life

Contents

Preface   ix

Memoirs
A Lost Traveller's Dream   3
The Fugitive, 1922-1925:
    A Personal Recollection Twenty Years After   24
The Gaze Past, the Glance Present:
    Forty Years After *The Fugitive*   35
Reflections on the Death of John Crowe Ransom   39
Miss Toklas' American Cake   46
Memories of Sylvia Beach   67
John Peale Bishop   69
Homage to St-John Perse   76
William Faulkner 1897-1962   82
Homage to T. S. Eliot   87

Opinions
Robert Frost as Metaphysical Poet   95
Introduction to *White Buildings* by Hart Crane   110
The Poetry of Edgar Allan Poe   115
A Note on Paul Valéry   128
Shadow: A Parable and a Polemic   140
Faulkner's *Sanctuary* and the Southern Myth   144
Three Commentaries: Poe, James, and Joyce   155
Humanism and Naturalism   170
Translation or Imitation?   195

Epilogue
A Sequence of Stanzas
    Compiled and Read to a Group of Friends
    on My Seventy-Fifth Birthday   211

Acknowledgments   217
Index   219

Preface

IN 1966 I decided to write an entire book of memories, and I was persuaded by certain friends that my "prodigious memory" would make the task an easy one. After I had written, with considerable difficulty, "A Lost Traveller's Dream" and "Miss Toklas' American Cake," I decided to try something else—what, I couldn't then be sure. My memory became less and less prodigious: my account of my first year in Paris had to be "checked" twice for the exposure of seventeen errors of simple fact. But this is not the principal reason why I decided to halt the memoir.

The "real" reason was that, unlike Ernest Hemingway in *A Moveable Feast*, I couldn't bring myself to tell what was wrong with my friends—or even mere aquaintances—without trying to tell what was wrong with myself. I am not sure, even now, what was, or is, wrong with me, and I was unwilling to give the reader the chance to make up his own mind on this slippery matter. Then, too, I fell back on authority: I couldn't let myself indulge in the terrible fluidity of self-revelation.

Nevertheless, there are memories in this book, but not all

of them written for this book. The first one was written thirty-three years ago, the last six months ago.

My preceding prose book, *Essays of Four Decades*, has a limited focus; that is, it is concerned with poetry and fiction as actualizations of culture; the focus of attention is severe. Having given up the systematic memoir, I saw an opportunity to revive several essays of a less formal, less severe purpose. *Essays of Four Decades* contains about forty essays. When the book was published, a young friend asked me, "Have you written just *one* essay a year for forty years?" No, I said—but I couldn't remember exactly how many I had written. I soon looked up the record. Going back to the nineteen-twenties and thirties when I was a free-lance literary journalist, I counted up through 1974; the result: 119 essays, including review-essays, two Swiftian satires, and a few old-fashioned personal essays.

The reader, if I have any, may well ask by what *criteria* (a favorite critical blur) I chose the contents of this book from three or four times the number of essays available in buried numbers of magazines, most of which are no longer published. The candid answer, bypassing attempts at principled objectivity, is that I do not know. The nearest to an objective standard was simply to ask this question of each possible title: will a reader today *understand* a certain essay, written five or even forty years ago, and if he understands, will what he understands extend or deepen his awareness? Awareness of what? That is the problem; for often an awareness of a hitherto unperceived quality in a poem by Donne or Stevens will mysteriously increase one's perceptiveness in a gallery filled with pictures by Miro or Klee. At this obscure stage of one's development one says, at least for a second time, that one doesn't know. Or I might change the point of view and say quite plainly: I thought a sufficient number of essays good enough for a book.

I am reviving, in this book, an old essay, "Humanism and Naturalism," an attack on the humanism of Norman Foerster, Irving Babbitt, and Paul Elmer More. The essay created something of a furor when it appeared in Eliot's *The Criterion* in July 1929, and in the *Hound and Horn* for Winter 1930. Its title then was "The Fallacy of Humanism." Eliot wrote me that he thought my essay a "brilliant article." It may be—or may have been. I saw very sharply what was wrong with the neo-Humanists because I had already seen it in myself without acknowledging it: a philosophy of literature that had no validity without religious authority to sustain it. The essay, looked at from this angle, is an attack on myself; but it was easier to project it onto others.

ALLEN TATE
February 27, 1975
Sewanee, Tennessee

I
MEMOIRS

To Malcolm Cowley

A Lost Traveller's Dream

1972

> ... *thou art still*
> *The son of morn in weary night's decline,*
> *The lost traveller's dream under the hill.*

A
S I BEGIN to write this sentence, I cannot foresee what kind of book will follow. I know only that it will not be an autobiography, but rather recollections of the "literary life" as I have seen it in the past fifty years in the United States and in some five years of living in Europe as a literary tourist, as a sometime lecturer, and as a half-hearted expatriate. Autobiography would demand more of myself than I know; it is easier to know other people than oneself because one may observe them; for one can but observe oneself, like André Gide, gazing daily into a looking-glass, a way to self-knowledge from which I should recoil. I shall be concerned with people in places and times: with friends who tried to teach me the art of poetry, which I could never quite learn, and with later friends who gave me the courage (if I may call it that) to live into middle and now into old age. These friends, some living, others dead, beckon me, of my will, not theirs, to account for as much of what I owe them as I shall be able to remember. What does one remember? How does one remember it? Vanity, pride, and fear are the obstacles to the recollection of persons and events that one knew only the year before last.

3

If the year before last is hard to remember, or if remembered, then remembered as not quite one's own year, what can one make of the palimpsest of one's life sixty years ago, each layer of which looks like a language different from all the others? To bring the past up to an intelligible pattern is a labor of the imagination. But imagination must take what is precariously, or even delusively, offered it, for the obstacles that I have spoken of deprive it of freedom of choice. Pride will keep me from exploring motives and actions that have colored my private life and inevitably affected the verse, criticism, and fiction that I have tried to write. Pride or shame? The French *pudeur* means both shame and modesty. Should one be immodest enough to try to tell all? That would be shameful. Let the authenticity of fact remain shadowy, as Henry James might have said, for however truthful the memorialist may try to be, his anecdotal recollections will be closer to fiction than to history.

One's awareness of this dilemma, history or fiction, or the treacherous interplay of both, is one's *selva obscura*. In the Dark Wood modern man may scarcely hope to find Vergil— merely Horatio, one's *alter ego* who is not "passion's slave" and who survives along with oneself "to tell my story." Horatio, at any rate, is the best narrator I have been able to find to allay the incredulity of the reader, if not my own. If I cannot wholly accept the order of what I think I remember, can I expect anybody else to accept it? I am therefore asking the reader of this book, if it shall have a reader, to think of what I shall tell him not as simple truth, but as "signatures" pointing to persons and events once as real as Johnson's cane tapping the pavement, but now faded into another kind of reality that will be perhaps in sight, but always a little beyond my reach.

Before I begin my story, before the first Once-upon-a-Time, I must beg the reader's further indulgence. I cannot believe that I differ from other American writers of my generation who used a respectable myth to deceive themselves and their readers into believing that they sprang fully equipped, like

Athene, from the head of Zeus. We didn't need to learn from
other writers what they had worked to acquire. If we owe a
great deal to James or Ford, we may appear to owe them less
if we acknowledge debts to writers to whom we owe very little.
Ernest Hemingway said that he had got everything from
Huckleberry Finn. He told me in the late twenties that he
couldn't understand the "dialect" of rural Arkansas, his wife
Pauline's native state; but if he couldn't understand the
Southwestern vernacular, he couldn't have understood Huck
Finn's speech well enough to use it. Before the generous ac-
knowledgment of Mark Twain's influence was widely known,
John Peale Bishop told me that Hemingway, in Paris in the
early twenties, read and reread Captain Marryat's *Peter
Simple,* and kept on his night-table for several months Defoe's
Captain Singleton. At about that same time, Ford Madox
Ford convinced me, for a while, because he had convinced himself, that he had got his prose style from Samuel Smiles, with
some influence from William Cobbett's *Rural Rides.* I have
occasionally told people who ask questions, but care little what
answer they get, that as a young man I tried to learn how to
write verse from James Thomson (B.V.), author of *The City
of Dreadful Night.* It would be disconcerting if there were
more truth in this than I can allow myself to believe fifty years
later.

If I were writing an autobiography the best I could do
would be to begin with a prenatal incident, such as the attack
by a bloodhound that my mother suffered a few months before I was born, and end (like Tristram Shandy) with my
birth. But it would be as difficult to begin with my birth as to
end with it. Until I was thirty I didn't know where I was born.
I thought I knew, and that might have been as good as knowing, had I not been suddenly confronted with the "truth." The
consequences of this confrontation were not as serious as the

dire recognition and reversal undergone by a Greek when he learned that he had been born in Thebes, and not as he had been led to believe, in defiance of the gods, in Corinth. Yet the shock was great, all the greater because at the moment of truth it would have been improper to show it.

I suppose one ought to consider it an advantage to have been born in one place up to the age of thirty, and for the next forty years to have been born in another. Two birthplaces, as I look back, prefigured my peregrinative childhood, for until I was thirty I never lived in one place longer than three years. For men of my region and time one's birthplace was important. "Place" was important. Edgar Poe, surely the least Bostonian man of his time in the United States, signed his first book "By a Bostonian" because, although Poe and Boston enjoyed mutual dislike, he had been born there. I have never felt like a Virginian—whatever it is to feel like a Virginian— and it was a relief, accompanied by a fleeting sense of bi-location, to learn that I had been born in Kentucky.

My mother had died at Monteagle, Tennessee, in July 1929, while I was in France. In the summer of 1930 I drove from Montgomery County, Tennessee, to Lexington, Kentucky, to meet my father and to carry him to Ashland in eastern Kentucky to visit my elder brother Varnell, who had just returned to Kentucky after some twenty years in the Southwest. I too had just come back to the South, having been away six years in New York and in Europe, and was set up in a beautiful old farmhouse on the south bank of the Cumberland River three miles from the tobacco town of Clarksville. My other brother, Benjamin—or just Ben as he was always known—had bought the place and given it to me, but kept the title in his name lest I sell it in hard times and live up the money. (When the place was sold in 1946 he gave me the money to buy another house.) In the South, houses too fine for the financial resources of the owners were often called "follies"; hence the name of that house: Benfolly, or Ben's Folly. Our friends said it was *his* folly to buy the house for me.

My daughter Nancy, then five years old, was with me in the rattly Model-A Ford. We met my father at the Phoenix Hotel in Lexington, and proceeded at once eastward towards Winchester. That town, eighteen miles east of Lexington, is the county seat of Clark County, a tobacco town like all the other Blue Grass county towns. About two miles from Winchester my father said, "Do you recognize that house?" He pointed north towards a square, red brick house, of no identifiable architecture, on a low hill some three hundred yards from the road. I did recognize it, for we had lived there occasionally from my earliest recollection until I was about ten; and there I had let a Negro boy, my playmate, take a beating from his mother, our cook Nanny, for a petty theft that I had committed. (Henry was killed in World War I; I never made it up to him for my cowardice.) As I slowed down to gaze at the house I felt an obscure agitation. I had not lived in Kentucky after I was sixteen, and I knew I would never live in Kentucky again. We sometimes moved two or three times a year, moving *away* from something my mother didn't like; or perhaps withdrawing would be a better word; for my mother gradually withdrew from the world, and withdrew me also, gradually, from the time I was a small boy; so that we might as well have been living, and I been born, in a tavern at a crossroads.

In a few minutes we were in Winchester, on Lexington Avenue, and my father asked me to slow down. Again he pointed to the north. "You were born in that house." It was a small, one-story white frame house. He explained that my mother wanted to be in town near the doctor in case I arrived in the middle of the night, for country roads in November were full of mud-holes. But that was all he said. If I said anything, I don't remember it. When we came to Mt. Sterling, the next county seat, I asked him about the lynching I had seen when I was eleven. He said he didn't remember the details. The day was hot and muggy. My little girl said, "Daddo, I wish we hadn't tooken this trip."

Had we not taken that trip I should be thinking to this day

that I had been born in Fairfax County, Virginia, for that was
where my mother said I was born, and she always bent reality
to her wishes. My father would not have forced upon me his
revised version of my birth; that was not his way; but he could
do it casually, as if, when we drove through Winchester, I were
a sightseer and he my guide. A few months later I told my
brother Ben that I felt I had been the victim of a shell-game.
He said, "You *were*. Forget it. We knew it all along."

My mother was born Eleanor Varnell a few months after the
surrender at Appomattox, whether in Prince William or Fairfax County, Virginia, I cannot be sure. I am not certain that
she knew; she may have been born in her father's Washington
house, which stood at the corner of Eleventh Street and Massachusetts Avenue until about 1890, when it was razed and
replaced by an apartment house. The house where she might
have been born, Pleasant Hill, was burnt to the ground by
General Blencker's New York "Dutch" Brigade on July 17,
1861, as the Union Army was advancing to fight the first
Battle of Manassas. The only other "big house" on her grandfather's farm was not in Fairfax, but over the Prince William
County line—a two-story hewn-log house called Chestnut Hill,
very old, which had been built by an early Lewis who had got
the land on a Fairfax grant warrant about 1750. From the
time I was six or seven years old I remember this old house;
for it was there that my mother took me to see our cousins,
children of her first cousin, Catherine Lewis Butt, who was
almost a generation older than my mother and who had been
present at the looting and burning of Pleasant Hill.

I remember being taken, when I was about ten or eleven, a
couple of miles from Chestnut Hill to see the foundations of
Pleasant Hill. The foundations, overrun with honeysuckle and
the poisonous jimson weed, appropriately a variety of night-
shade, looked like polished marble (or so I was told), at one

end of which remained the stump of a large, crumbling brick chimney. I was shown the spot, out back near the milk-house, where Cousin Catherine's mother, my great-aunt Anna, just missed being shot by a drunken Yankee soldier who was chasing a pig to get close enough to shoot it. Aunt Anna bravely (or so I was told) stood between the pig and the soldier, who fired his rifle through her voluminous skirts (between her legs, though these were never mentioned in the hundreds of times I heard the story), without wounding her, but killing the pig.

Pleasant Hill was about eight miles east of Fairfax Station on the Ox Road, a "corduroy road" which was so slow that the eight miles needed more than two hours of bumps from one log to the next laid across the road at right angles. In the summer of 1913 the black boy who was driving the surrey grunted with each bump, and my mother at short intervals reproved him, saying, "Stop that." "Yes'm," he would say, and then to the horse, "Giddap!" And we bumped faster. At Sangster's Crossroads we turned uphill into a muddy lane which ran a quarter of a mile to the site of Pleasant Hill. On the left, as we ascended, was a line of ancient, gnarled cedars which wound with the lane. Twenty-five years later, at a party in Washington, a lady liked my gold studs and asked if she might hold one of them in her hand. I handed it to her. She clasped it for a silent minute, then said: "The original owner was a small man with bushy white hair and a hawk's nose, formal and pompous; he lived in a big frame house on a hilltop, which one reached by a lane bordered on one side by cedar trees." As I write these words the *frisson* of that moment returns. I asked her how she knew. She replied that she didn't know; something else knew; she was a psychometrist. The first owner of the studs, from whom through several other hands they were passed on to me, was the prototype of Major Lewis Buchan of my novel *The Fathers*. What the psychometrist had told me was that Pleasant Hill had somewhere an objective existence almost a century after it was burnt, when it could still be known by a person who had never seen or heard of it. The next year I began to write the novel. Any table rapper could have conjured up from the 1850s a man with bushy white hair and pompous manners: such men were all over the place, from Boston to New Orleans. Few such men had a lane winding uphill and bordered on one side only by cedars. I accept, but neither believe nor disbelieve the psychometric revelation that made it possible for me to write my novel. I have not had another revelation and I have not written another novel.

I remember the summer of 1907, the year of the Jamestown Exposition, which my mother had to see "because we are descended from Jamestown"; so after a few weeks at Virginia Beach we went to Jamestown; but I don't remember anything I saw there. I am sure I am not descended from any 1607 settler of Jamestown, yet my mother's belief took on in my mind years later a certain plausibility. Judging by the behavior of some of her uncles and brothers, I decided that we could have as an ancestor the unhappy "gentleman" who in that first grim winter of famine ate the corpse of his wife. Captain John Smith's entire shipload were gentlemen of the kidney that would not allow them to demean themselves with manual labor, even to live. My mother believed in heredity. I can think of no ancestor for two of her brothers more suitable than the gentleman cannibal of Jamestown, so perhaps we go back to 1607 after all.

That same summer we proceeded to Washington where I saw and now remember vividly my great-uncle Samuel Bogan, one of three brothers who became doctors, two in Washington, and one in Illinois after the Civil War. Uncle Sam had gone with the Union as a surgeon in the Army of the Potomac, and at Gettysburg must have dressed the wounds of brothers and cousins captured at the end of Pickett's charge. I can't remember what he looked like then; years later I saw a photograph in which the leonine, or perhaps merely bushy, grey hair told me he was a son of Pleasant Hill.

In 1955 I visited Uncle Sam's son, Cousin Fred, then eighty-five, in California where the family had migrated in 1907, his father having retired; that must have been soon after our visit at the old house in Washington. I remember the dark parlor and the dingy horsehair furniture, and family portraits high on the walls, some of them my own forbears, cracked and dim as the past of which, now almost seventy years later, they have become a private symbol.

Cousin Fred told me that a few weeks before the trek to California his father had asked him to come out into the backyard to help him dispose of a fifty years' accumulation of old letters and papers. But Cousin Fred was not to help; he was to witness. His father, standing before the incinerator, asked him to look at a batch of papers, saying bitterly that here was the family fortune, and then throwing them angrily into the fire. The papers were $150,000 in Confederate bonds. Uncle Sam, the Unionist, was bitter because his father had supported a cause which he, Uncle Sam, had rejected, and had thus thrown away his and his brothers' patrimony. I have a letter written by Major Bogan to his daughter, my grandmother, a year after the burning of Pleasant Hill, in which the old man said that were he not so old (he was sixty-eight) he would enlist as a private in the Confederate Army. In my novel I made him a Unionist for the sake of the plot, history seldom being as dramatic as one would like it to be; and I think Cousin Fred, when he read the novel, didn't like that part of it, because in retrospect he felt like a Confederate, in defiance of his father's Unionist anger and the worthless Confederate bonds.

On these visits to Virginia and Washington I saw many other relations, but being little concerned with myself after my boyhood, I shall be trying in this memoir to find out what made me the kind of writer I am. Of this enquiry I can scarcely expect success, for the reader may discover between the lines motives and explanations that I thought I had concealed or forgotten. Poets, perhaps even more than novelists, are not unlike hunters who stand in tall weeds, waiting for the dove to fly from the field of millet to the water in the creek which will renew her life; and then we blaze away and the dove drops in the weeds on our side of the field. One September day in the valley below Sewanee, twenty-five years ago, I shot a dove that fell into the weeds, and when I found her she was lying head up with a gout of blood in each eye. I shot her again. Her life had been given to my memory; and I have never hunted from that day.

Memory arrests the flow of inner time, but what we remember is not at the command of our wills; it has its own life and purposes; it gives what *it* wills. St. Augustine tells us that memory is like a woman. The Latin *memoria* is properly a feminine noun, for women never forget; and likewise the soul is the *anima*, even in man, his vital principle and the custodian of memory, the image of woman that all men both pursue and flee. The feminine memory says: Here is that dying dove; you must really kill it this time or you will not remember it from all the other birds you have killed; take it or leave it; I have given it to you. The imaginative writer is the archeologist of memory, dedicated to the minute particulars of the past, definite things—*prima sacrimenti memoria*. If his "city" is to come alive again from a handful of shards, he will try to fit them together in an elusive jigsaw puzzle, most of the pieces of which are forever lost.

An incident of 1912 or 1913 gave me, as I began later to fit it into a pattern, a glimpse of the past that reversed my stance at the time it happened. Instead of looking back, I felt that I had been shifted into the past and was looking into a future that nobody but myself at the end of the eighteenth century could have seen. The incident was an afternoon visit to a personage whom I had heard spoken of as "Aunt Martha

Jackson." The visit had been arranged a few days before by Aunt Martha's granddaughter, a tall dignified mulatto who seemed to have time for sewing and other little tasks for my mother. I was ordered to address her as Aunt Atha. She came to our "residence hotel"—a designation which in those days meant a respectable boardinghouse for reduced gentility—in Logan Circle, and escorted us to her grandmother's house, a long street-car ride to northeast Washington.

Small, battened, and unpainted, the house stood back a few steps from a white-washed picket fence along which grew hollyhocks, castor beans, and sunflowers. The old woman, dressed in black, sat in a low rocking chair. The white-washed walls were spotless, like the immaculate old woman. She had a fixed gaze into space: I knew that she was blind. "Is that Nellie Varnell?" she said—not "Miss Nellie." My mother said, "Yes, ma'am." She went to the old woman, bent over and kissed the high, pale yellow forehead. The next thing I remember I was being pushed forward and made to sit in a split-bottom chair, facing the old lady. Her sagging skin, too large for her shrunken flesh, had the dull patina of dried mullein; her hair was straight and snow-white. She ran her bird-like claws over my forehead, my ears, my nose, my chin. I was more embarrassed than frightened, and I wanted to get up, but I sat until my mother touched my shoulder; I rose and backed away. Aunt Martha said, "He favors his grandpa." I can still hear her voice, high and weak. It was Tidewater, not Negro. My recollection ends with the resemblance to my grandfather, which the old lady could see through the bony ends of her talons.

She must have meant my great-grandfather, in whose family she had been a slave; but I didn't look like him either, as I knew later from a daguerreotype. I doubt that she thought so; she was only making me a member of the family, accepting me with the aristocratic courtesy that survived with some former slaves longer than their masters could keep it. As we left, my mother said she had forgotten how old Aunt Martha was. Atha said that mammy was about a hundred and twenty because she remembered General Washington's funeral. To remember in 1913 a funeral in 1799 she must have been older than a hundred and twenty, having been born not much later than 1790. She had been my great-grandmother's maid; she was also, according to legends I heard later, my great-grandfather's half-sister, the daughter of Dr. John Armistead Bogan (1766-1814) by a slave-woman he had bought in the West Indies. If the sense of a past comes less from parish registers, old houses, family Bibles, old letters, county records, and tombstones, than from the laying on of hands from one generation to another, then what sense of a living past I may have goes back through the bird-claws of an ancient female slave, my blood-cousin who, ironically enough, in family authority seemed to take precedence over my mother.

It was late in the afternoon of August 5, 1914 (how I remember the date will presently become clear), and I was fourteen years old. My mother and I were staying at an old-fashioned summer resort, a "chatauqua," Mountain Lake Park in western Maryland, where daily concerts and lectures, and Sunday sermons, edified the hours not given to immemorable conversation on the verandahs of hotels and boarding-houses. Every summer we had to get away from the oppressive heat of Kentucky. We never quite got away from it, for that summer we had already tried and found wanting in salubrity two other resorts in the mountains of Virginia of which I remember nothing but their evocative names—Nimrod Hall and Sweet Chalybeate Springs. So we made the rounds of the mountain resorts every summer, and of some that weren't in the mountains— Dawson Springs and Crab Orchard in Kentucky, where the spring water was usually cold but the air hot and muggy; even swooping down to Estill Springs at the foot of the Cumberland Mountains in Tennessee. But after I was six we didn't go to Estill. My mother's friend, "Miss Maria," who was to be the grandmother of the second Mrs. Douglas MacArthur, had died some years before, and my mother didn't quite like the "Beard House" after her death. Yet Estill Springs had an indirect influence on my life, for it was there that my elder brothers, in the late nineties and early 1900s, made the friends who persuaded them to go to Vanderbilt, instead of the University of Kentucky or the University of Virginia. Had they not gone to Vanderbilt I should probably have followed them wherever they had gone, and I should not be writing this book, and should not have written any books. I should have liked that, provided I could have liked what I might have done instead. The only person to whom one's writings are indispensable is oneself, for a few days after they are written.

August 5, 1914, was a hot day. Late in the afternoon I was playing mixed doubles on a badly kept tennis court where wire-grass sprouted under the net and the chicken-wire backstops had so many holes that I had to chase the balls while my pretty partner, dressed in middy blouse and blue skirt well below her knees, took for granted my role of *cavalière servente*. She was a slender blonde and she had what was called in that era "poise," and I was eager to please her by winning the set with my new Lawford stroke. She was a year older than I and had a beau (or so she said) who would be a freshman at Charlottesville next month. Several times a day, usually after "dinner," at twelve-thirty, when we played Hearts or Five Hundred for an hour before nap time, she said that Pendy (possibly Pendleton something) was already being rushed by the Dekes. My lame reply to this was that I might someday be a Phi because my brothers were, and I put my age up a year quite plausibly because I was tall for my age and had been recently promoted to long trousers. But I must have known that I was not getting very far with—well, I can't remember her name. Yet August 5, 1914, brings her back to me in that nodule of memory where boyish love and the rumor of war are joined; and I think of her as Miss Science Hill. That was the name of

her boarding-school in Kentucky, which I could match with
the Cross School in Louisville in that adolescent snobbery by
which the young place each other. I had known for several
days that I was getting nowhere with my lines from the poets,
which I recited to her or wrote out and asked a cooperative
waiter to put under her plate at supper. One evening, when my
mother had "retired" with a sick headache, and Miss Science's
parents were away, perhaps at Deer Park where there was a
racetrack, I tried her with a few lines from "The Skeleton in
Armor"—rather poor strategy since she must have known
that I was not thinking of her but just showing off. Shelley's
"Love's Philosophy" was equally futile, even

>   All things by a law divine
>   In one another's being mingle—
>   Why not I with thine?

   Like turning cartwheels or doing backflips, I must have let
her—or if not her, other girls somewhere else when I was that
age—I must have let her in for my entire repertory of verse,
which included lines from "The Rape of Lucrece." I was be-
guiled by the naughty title when I read it at age eleven or
twelve in the dingy back parlor in Clark County, in the one-
volume Shakespeare which was bound in buckram and gilt and
which I am sure nobody else had looked at for years. Had I not
won a prize in "elocution" for my recitation of "The Skeleton
in Armor"? I may have favored Miss Science Hill with Poe's
"To Helen," which along with "The Sleeper" I had read many
times in one of the three volumes of Poe that, according to a
signature on a flyleaf, had belonged to my great-grandfather
in Virginia, Major Bogan.
   I must have made an effort to memorize poems, but I only
remember reciting them, often on inauspicious occasions, as
when my mother was present. She was what was called in
those days an "inveterate reader," but she disapproved of my
reading. One day when I was about twelve, leaning against the

newel post in the front hall in Clark County, reading *Through the Looking-Glass,* or perhaps *Miss Minerva and William Green Hill,* my mother said, "Son, put that book down and go out and play with Henry. You are straining your mind and you know your mind isn't very strong." So, at the age when most boys turned backflips to impress the girls, I was quoting poetry to them as surrogates of my mother, to whom I had to prove that I was not an imbecile.

My mother was both restless and restive, constantly moving about, Louisville to Clark County to Washington to Nashville (where my older brothers were in college); then the circuit was repeated many times, with epicycles into southern Illinois where she had cousins and where she had spent some years right after she and my father were married. I am afraid to try to count up the number of schools I went to all told, lest I suffer the humiliation of forgetting a few of them.

But I am still at Mountain Lake Park, on the tennis court with Miss Science Hill. I remember few incidents of my boyhood as well as that set of tennis, and I should like to think that the pretty blonde is now the mnemonic trigger of my memory. It was rather what broke up the game that brings the scene back to me.

A grown man, possibly the father of one of our opponents, strode out onto the court waving a newspaper. We gathered around him. It was the *Washington Post* for that morning, August 5, 1914, and he had got it off the westbound Baltimore and Ohio train. The headlines read somewhat as follows: VON MOLTKE INVADES BELGIUM GERMANS SWEEP ALL BEFORE THEM LIEGE BESIEGED.

What effect could a war in Europe have on me? No more than the news of a thunderstorm over at Deer Park. I could not know that August 5, 1914, was the end of the nineteenth century, and that four years later, when I entered college, I would be in a new world so different from the old that I would never quite understand it, but would be both of it and opposed to it the rest of my life.

When I learned to read I can't remember; I do remember reading, a few months before I was six, a child's version of selections from *The Arabian Nights;* and, being a credulous child, I was certain that the gigantic bird, the roc, lifted Sinbad out of the Valley of Diamonds. There was also a child's history of the French Revolution that I read at about the same time, while I was in bed with chicken pox, calling out to my mother to ask the meaning of certain words, of which I could spell out the letters. I remember the gaudy color illustrations, one being of Marie Antoinette with her head on the block and the blade about to fall, her long blonde tresses streaming over the block like a cascade in sunlight. How my mother had taught me to read I don't know, and I doubt that she could have explained how. Her own education, like her charity, had begun at home, and was finished at the Convent of the Visitation in Georgetown in the early 1880s, where, according to an old "certificate" I found after her death, she had "studied" drawing and painting, rhetoric, French, music, and ballroom dancing, though this must have been under chaperonage outside the convent.

My first reading was in the fall of 1906 in the Tulane Hotel in Nashville. My mother had taken the Boys (I was never one of the Boys, merely Allen) to enter them in college. After chicken pox I had in succession measles and scarlet fever, which kept me in bed, where my mother didn't object to having me, and I read or she read to me *Grimm's Fairy Tales*, Hans Christian Andersen, Henty's *With Clive in India* and *With Lee in Virginia*. I liked best of all Page's *Two Little Confederates*, the heroes of which I envied the blue, double-barreled guns sent them after the war by the wounded Yankee they had helped to nurse back to life in their farm house. Some time that winter I read *Undine*, and reread it often until I went to college; I have wondered if the water imagery in my verse goes back to it, since I have little experience of the ocean, being an inlander. Through the years of my childhood my mother's favorite authors were Scott—but neither

Dickens nor Thackeray—Mary Johnston, John Esten Cooke, E. P. Roe, Henry Sydnor Harrison, James Lane Allen, and Augusta Evans, author of *St. Elmo,* of whom it was said that she had swallowed an unabridged dictionary. I read most of these novelists, and others besides: *When Knighthood Was in Flower* (I've forgotten who wrote it), *The Three Musketeers* and *The Vicomte de Bragelonne,* and the Oz books.

I can't remember how old I was when I read certain books. Those I have mentioned, and many others, including some of the Nick Carter dime novels, I read before I was fourteen. I doubt that by becoming a bookworm I "proved" anything to my mother: she seldom saw what she had decided not to see. If she wanted me to "go out and play," there were few playmates; very few children got through the fine mesh of her screen. After I was at last allowed to go to school I had to prove myself in a different direction, where stood, some distance away, boys of my own age. I was always the "new boy" at school. Years later I saw myself as Charles Bovary, the awkward, self-conscious new boy entering the hostile class and timidly blushing. I had to win my masculine standing at every new school by fist-fighting the bully. I don't think I ever won, for if my mind was weak, my physique was weaker; and I usually came off with a torn shirt or a bloody nose. But there were other ways of being a man which obviated physical combat. About six months before we went to Mountain Lake Park I was fourteen, and was given long trousers on my birthday. I must have decided to seize at once a prerogative of the *toga virilis.*

I am sure I planned every step. After dinner, which we had at midday, the young members of the family went to the head of the table, shook hands with my father, and thanked him for the meal. He then got up and went silently towards the back of the house to a small room called the Office, the furnishings of which were a swivel chair and a dusty rolltop desk. He put his hat down on his nose and went immediately to sleep. When I could hear him snore I crept into the room, lifted the key to the sideboard from his vest pocket, crept back into the dining room, unlocked the lower door, and grabbed the quart bottle. Out in the stable, my two friends and I drank very little of it. I had taken rock-candy soaked in whiskey, but this was the first time I had drunk whiskey straight; I gagged and spat it out. I ran back to replace the bottle, went to the Office and slid the key into the pocket from which I should not have taken it.

All seemed to go well. After a few days of the handshaking ritual I felt I was in the clear. Then one day after I had thanked him for dinner, he gestured for me to wait. He was a large, handsome man, about six feet, whose eyes were blue, cold, and expressionless. I was afraid of him; I never stopped being afraid of him, for he always spoke to me impersonally as if he were surprised that I was there. He gave me a fishy stare, straight through me, and said, "Son, the next time you steal the whiskey, don't ruin it for other people by filling up the bottle with water." There was a moral in it, but I didn't know then and I am not sure now what it was: possibly that only low whites and Negroes stole whiskey and that drinking must not be secret. It, too, was a public, ritualistic act, and it followed that I had to be humiliated before company at dinner.

He had humiliated me before—but he didn't know that he had—when I was about eight years old in Nashville. One morning a letter arrived that upon reading my mother burst into tears and left the room. I seized the wicked sheet of paper and threw it into the fire. When she returned a few minutes later, perfectly composed, she glanced at me, then at the fireplace, and said, "Son, why did you do that?" Years later I asked my mother why she didn't get a divorce, and she replied, as if she were governed by a natural law, that ladies of her generation didn't get divorces. And years later than that conversation my brother Ben told me that our father had been asked in 1905 to resign from a men's club, having laughed at the mention of a certain woman's name at a club dinner. My father's "withdrawal" from social life was even more extreme than my mother's, or seemed so. I didn't know who his friends were or where they were. I still do not know whether my mother's perpetual motion was flight from her husband, or whether his long absences were flights from her.

The family had been living on land with a vengeance, by selling it off a parcel at a time until the time when I entered college and it was almost all gone, except a few slum houses that my mother owned in Washington. My father's lumber business was always a little vague, for we never lived where it was; and after about 1910 or 1911 he had no business. After his death in 1933 I found some worthless stock certificates amounting to about $40,000 dollars, of the Ruthven Railway Signal Company. A man named Ruthven had invented a foolproof device to prevent all railroad wrecks; it only remained, to make the stockholders millionaires, to persuade all the railroads to lay down new tracks from New York to San Francisco, and from Chicago to New Orleans.

Of my mother's two sisters and three brothers, one sister was evidently a fine woman who died young; but the other siblings were a little strange, and doubtless gave my mother reason to think that one of her sons might have a weak mind. She was haunted by the brother and sister who had to be put away, but I never heard that they fell into melancholia because of excessive application to books. She had two other brothers, descendants surely of the Jamestown cannibal, whom she seldom mentioned—the one a drunkard and follower of the horses, the other a petty embezzler who had more money than he stole paid out to lawyers to keep him out of jail, and who was quietly rumored to have married a whore in St. Louis and then to have vanished into the Far West forever. The strange sister married a Creole from Louisiana who took her on their honeymoon to the St. Charles Hotel in New Orleans, where he pushed her down an elevator shaft, or was said by her family to have done this: they didn't like Mr. Archambault, who of course spoke English with a French accent and was therefore a foreigner. Aunt Daisy was put away after this unhappy marriage. Mr. Archambault was not heard from again.

The uncle who fell into melancholy in his teens never drank or smoked, nor ever, my father said after my mother's death, had carnal knowledge of woman; and being the youngest child he had slept with his mother until he was twelve years old, the old lady having banished her husband from her bed after Uncle Leo's birth. I remember seeing Uncle Leo only once, when I was about thirteen, in Ashland, where he had stopped off to see "Sister Nellie" on his way to Texas. He was a tall man, very thin, "jimber-jawed," with large, liquid, burning eyes, who read nothing but the Bible and crank religious tracts. His manner was affable and considerate; my mother said he was her only brother who was a true gentleman. After his visit with us he went on to Caldwell County, Texas, where he bought some land and oil leases which he was never able to develop. He had a "mental breakdown" and died in an institution thirty years later.

A few weeks after I had heard from a cousin that he was dead, I saw myself sitting on one end of a log and, on the other, Uncle Leo. We were in a thicket of scrub oaks. He was on the end of the log near the road, beyond which stood a four-story brick apartment house in which I lived on the top floor. There was no other building in sight. As I looked at Uncle Leo he fixed me with his large, brown, opaque eyes, and I was afraid of him. To get to my apartment across the the road I must somehow circumvent him, so I got up slowly, then began to run as fast as I could behind his back to the house, dashed in, and got into the elevator, satisfied that I had outwitted a demon. He could not pursue me up the stairs as fast as the elevator would take me to my flat. At the top floor I opened the elevator door. There stood Uncle Leo barring my way. I have never understood how this poor man could play such an important part in my secret life. He was not only a gentleman, but gentle; ruined by a powerful, matriarchal mother. I have had few other dreams that I can remember in such perfect detail.

The Fugitive, 1922-1925

A Personal Recollection
Twenty Years After

1942

SOMETIME in November 1921 I was talking to Donald Davidson, then a young English instructor, on the front steps of old College Hall at Vanderbilt. After some casual talk Don told me that he and a few other men, including John Crowe Ransom, had been meeting at the house of a friend on every other Saturday night to read poems and to discuss "philosophy." He asked me to come the next time. I said that I would but I cannot remember whether I felt any excitement except in my own vanity, for Don and John were professors; and when I got there the next Saturday night, being the only undergraduate present, I was flattered. Who read poems I do not know; yet I seem to remember that Don read a long romantic piece called "The Valley of the Dragon," in which the monster shielded lovers from the world. I imitated it soon afterwards; but neither the original nor its echo was allowed to survive.

I remember the tone of the conversation; it was not very literary but philosophical and even philological, and I soon suspected why I had been asked to come. We had two hosts, Mr. James Frank, a cultivated businessman of Nashville, and his brother-in-law, Dr. Sidney Mttron Hirsch, a man of vast, if somewhat perverse, erudition; and it was plain that I had been invited to hear him talk. He was a mystic and I think a Rosicrucian, a great deal of whose doctrine skittered elusively among imaginary etymologies. At that time I was not very consciously a poet. I was studying Greek and Sanskrit, and if I had behaved myself I should no doubt have gone the next year to the American School in Athens. But I had not studied Hebrew, and I never knew what Dr. Hirsch's middle name, Mttron, meant; I understood that it might be an archangel. He was a large man, an invalid who never moved from his *chaise longue*, and he always presided at our meetings. On this first evening he asked me what I knew about the Trojan horse. My answer must have seemed to him ignorant, for he brushed it aside and went on to explain that *woode* in Middle English meant "mad," and that the Trojan horse being the wooden horse must be the mad horse; and that since madness is divine, the Trojan horse is the esoteric and symbolic horse. Shining pince-nez stood up on his handsome nose, and curled Assyrian hair topped a massive brow.

How many men were there that evening I cannot recall. (Until Laura Riding became a member of the group, after I had gone to live in New York, women were never present, only Mrs. Frank and Miss Hirsch, the philosopher's sister, coming in after the poems were all read to serve us an excellent supper.) Yet all that winter there was a constant attendance of some five or six men who ranged themselves somewhat formally round Dr. Hirsch's *chaise longue*.

By February or early March of 1922 the original "Fugitive group" was formed, although it had no name. There was Stanley Johnson, a man who would stand no nonsense from anybody and who wrote some good verse, and later wrote a novel about professors, having been one himself; but after the novel he never wrote anymore. Alec Stevenson had been in the war, and I think for a time he thought of being a teacher, but he went into business, and after the first year of our meetings wrote less and less; but he wrote some beautiful things that should have long ago gone into a book. The only academic scholar among us was Walter Clyde Curry, later the author of books on Chaucer and Shakespeare and of learned articles on medieval magic and astrology: he was a sympathetic friend and a sonneteer who could write good lines, but he was not committed to poetry. Some years later he neatly typed out his poems, had them bound, and gave them the title: "Futility, a Volume of Useless Verse." To these early meetings came also the Starr brothers, Milton and Alfred, the latter a good mathematician, and both well-read men. William Yandell Elliott and William Frierson, being away at Oxford as Rhodes scholars, were made members *in absentia*. There may have been casual visitors that first year but I cannot remember them.

Uppermost in my mind are Donald Davidson and John Crowe Ransom, who for me, at that early stage, meant just about everything. Don was writing what I suppose were his first poems; they were about lovers and dragons, and there was one about a tiger-woman that I thought was remarkable; but Don's own liking for this sort of thing declined at about the time mine did; and in the summer of 1922 he began to write poems that I think are still among his best. John Ransom always appeared at the Fugitive meetings with a poem (some of us didn't), and when his turn came he read it in a dry tone of understatement. I can only describe his manner in those days as irony which was both brisk and bland. Before we began to think of a magazine John had written a poem which foreshadowed the style for which he has become famous; it was "Necrological," still one of his best poems. I marvelled at it because it seemed to me that overnight he had left behind him the style of his first book and, without confusion, had mastered a new style. We all knew that John was far better than we were, and although he never asserted his leadership we looked to him for advice.

Soon after the first issue of *The Fugitive* appeared, I met Merrill Moore on the campus, and he astonished me by handing me a manuscript. It was a poem called "To a Fetish," his first, I believe, and in quatrains (five or six of them), a fact worth remarking since shortly afterwards he began to write only sonnets. I read the poem. "What do you think of it?" Merrill asked. "I think it is wonderful," I said. Then he asked me if I thought it would qualify him for "membership" in the group. I told him I was certain that it would. I took the poem to Donald Davidson, and Merrill came to the next meeting and to every other meeting I am sure until the group broke up. He quickly became the most prolific poet not only among us but probably in the world. He would read us his poems and we would criticize a line here and there, but he never acted upon our advice. It was easier for him to write a new poem than to revise an old one. To one meeting I believe he brought twenty-one poems, and he seldom brought fewer than ten. One of his poems was called "The Hackberry Tree"; it must have its claim to survival because although I have not seen it since the night he read it to us twenty years ago, I can remember it perfectly:

> The hackberry tree baffles me.
> I cannot tell whether the hackberry tree
> Is in the clouds, or whether the clouds
> Are in the hackberry tree.

But this is enough, lest Merrill do likewise by me. Eighteen years after *The Fugitive* appeared Merrill had written more than fifty thousand sonnets.

I have often been asked to tell how we got the magazine started, and why we called it *The Fugitive*. The man who first suggested that the poems we had been reading on alternate Saturday nights should be published in a magazine of our own, was our moderator, Dr. Hirsch; and it was he too who gave the magazine its name. As I have already said, we sat against the walls of Mr. Frank's living room and were presided over by Dr. Hirsch. He was always Doctor, as for that matter were we; attendance at the meetings seemed to confer upon us all the degree of Doctor, but Doctor of what I never knew. Dr. Hirsch asked us in turn to read our "offerings," as they were called, and when we had read he called for criticism. Carbon copies were always passed around in order to make possible minute criticism of every poem. Dr. Hirsch had an unfailing courtesy and elevation of tone, and when he came to me he usually lowered his head to his hand and waited patiently for it to be over. At that time I received only gentle comment (it soon changed!) doubtless because I was the only undergraduate and not much could be expected of me.

At a meeting like this, then, Dr. Hirsch proposed the magazine. It seemed to us all a project of the utmost temerity, if not of folly. This must have been sometime in February 1922. Our imminent folly alarmed not only us but our friends; I remember distinctly that Dr. Edwin Mims, head of the Vanderbilt English Department, a Southern Liberal of the old school and the boss of most of our group, invited us to lunch at a place called, I believe, the Commercial Club, and tried to persuade us to desist. A little later he praised us. But we went ahead. We found our printer, a Negro firm which did the work very cheap; but after the first issue, when we had subscribers and other backers, we got a better printer, Cullum and Ghertner, whose names should be recorded because they were patient with our finical corrections of proof and in waiting for their money. I write all this from memory, without references, so I do not remember when we received more substantial patronage; yet it was not long before the Associated Retailers of Nashville, a businessmen's organization headed by Mr. Jacques Back, began to give us a subsidy, which was continued to the end. *The Fugitive* was doubtless the only "little magazine" which suspended publication not for lack of funds but for lack of an editor. The time came when nobody could do the work.

Then Dr. Hirsch gave us the name: *The Fugitive.** It
turned out to be a good one because it invited ridicule. What
were we fleeing from? Or towards? Dr. Hirsch's most erudite
irony was turned upon these jests. For a Fugitive was quite
simply a Poet: the Wanderer, or even the Wandering Jew,
the Outcast, the man who carries the secret wisdom around
the world. It was a fairly heavy responsibility for us to undertake, but we undertook it, with the innocence of which only
the amateur spirit is capable.

All that remained now to be done was to select the poems
for the first issue, which we did with our usual formality,
by secret ballot, the result of which Donald Davidson still
has on the back of a letter from the late Chancellor Kirkland
of Vanderbilt telling Don that there were no University apart-
ments available to him—news which in those days might
have also told Don, if he needed telling, that he was indubit-
ably a poet. I was admitted to the first issue with two pre-
posterously bad poems, one of them about Sinbad the Sailor,
which had started out to be a long poem but which never got
beyond twenty lines.

We took pseudonyms, less for concealment, I believe, than
for the "romance"—as Ford Madox Ford said when I asked
him why he liked to raise hogs. The disguises were not without
humor and a certain judgment of ourselves. John's "Roger
Prim" needs no comment. Don's "Robin Gallivant" still tells
us something about that romantic poet. I don't know why
Merrill's "Dendric" fitted him perfectly; I always thought,
being an etymologist in those days, that it was the Greek
root for tree, with the "pertaining to" suffix, giving us Tree-
like or Tree-ish. But if Merrill was like a tree, the tree was
a dense fern tree of the primordial tropics. When I announced
that I was "Henry Feathertop"—from Hawthorne's story—
nobody objected. Nobody even smiled.

After the second issue—the first was in April 1922, the

---

*Some years later I learned that the late Alec B. Stevenson gave
our magazine its name.

second in June—we dropped the fancy names. Some of the New York reviewers had said that the first issue had been written by one man, and that man was John Ransom. So out of consideration for John's future reputation, and perhaps in some vanity of our own, we published a key to the *noms de plume* which is on record in the third issue of *The Fugitive* and elsewhere, if anybody is interested in it.

In May, a few weeks after the first number, a doctor sent me to the mountains of North Carolina for six months, so I did not graduate with my class in June. In the nine months of my absence from Nashville I think I began seriously to study the writing of poetry, and I began to be a little more aware of the world, or at any rate of the literary world, at large. In May, Hart Crane had seen one of my poems in *The Double Dealer*, a "little" *Dial* published in New Orleans. He wrote me a letter from Cleveland and sent me some back numbers of *The Little Review*. He said that my poem showed that I had read Eliot—which I had not done; but I soon did; and my difficulties were enormously increased. Anyhow from Eliot I went on to the other moderns, and I began to connect with the modern world what I had already learned from Baudelaire, first through Arthur Symons, then from Baudelaire himself. I mention this personal history because I believe it was through me that modern poetry made its first impact upon the doctors who gathered fortnightly in Mr. Frank's house. *The Waste Land* had come out by the time I went back to Nashville in February 1923. I began an impertinent campaign in Eliot's behalf in the South.

My conceit must have been intolerable. Had not the editors of *The Double Dealer* written me a letter saying that they saw in me the White Hope of the South? Add to that the easy lesson in shocking the bourgeoisie that I had learned from reading French poets, and was relearning for American use from Ezra Pound, and you have before you the figure of a twenty-two-year-old prig as disagreeable as you could possibly conjure up, until you see in him several varieties of snob-

bishness, when he becomes even more disagreeable. In that
moral condition I returned to Vanderbilt to get my degree.
I got it; but meanwhile I almost didn't get it, because my
career as a Fugitive had become, for me, more interesting
than ever. In my absence I had discovered that I was to be
a poet. I had tried a job in my brother's business in Kentucky
and found out that I could not be a businessman. My brother
had found it out at about the same time.

One day in February 1923 (I think it was) I was typing
a bad poem entitled "William Blake" on Walter Clyde Curry's
typewriter. Dr. Curry gave the poets the freedom of his
rooms. I became aware of a presence at my back and turning
round I saw the most remarkable-looking boy I had ever laid
eyes on. He was tall and thin, and when he walked across
the room he made a sliding shuffle, as if his bones didn't
belong to one another. He had a long quivering nose, large
brown eyes, and a long chin—all topped by curly red hair.
He spoke in a soft whisper, asking to see my poem; then he
showed me one of his own—it was about Hell, and I remember this line:

Where lightly bloom the purple lilies. . . .

He said that he was sixteen years old and a sophomore. This
remarkable young man was "Red," Robert Penn Warren, the
most gifted person I have ever known.

Red soon took me to see a friend of his who had come
back from the war to get his degree—had come, in fact,
glowing with the prestige of a first novel called *Hoax* which
I immediately read with admiration and envy but which I
have totally forgotten. This man was Ridley Wills, cousin of
Jesse Wills who had recently written some excellent sonnets
and had become a Fugitive. Two cousins were never more unlike. Jesse was tall, awkward, shy, and sensitive; Ridley was
small, graceful, ebullient, and arrogant, and one of the wittiest
and most amusing companions I have ever had. Red, Ridley,

and I joined up, and proceeded to get for the spring term room number 353 on the top floor of Wesley Hall, the theological building which bore over its portals the inscription: *Schola Prophetarum.* We named the architecture Methodist Gothic. It was no place for the heathen. Ten years later it burnt to the ground.

It was one large room with two double-decker beds, and Ridley and I being older than Red made him sleep above. In order to get into bed at night we had to shovel the books, trousers, shoes, hats, and fruit jars onto the floor, and in the morning, to make walking space, we heaped it all back upon the beds. We stuck pins into Red while he slept to make him wake up and tell us his dreams. Red had made some good black-and-white drawings in the Beardsley style. One day he applied art-gum to the dingy plaster and when we came back we saw four murals, all scenes from *The Waste Land.* I remember particularly the rat creeping softly through the vegetation, and the typist putting a record on the gramophone. Then one night in the spring Ridley and I went down to "the" dog-wagon and wrote by dawn the entire *Golden Mean.* When we showed the manuscript to Merrill Moore the next day, Merrill was pretty envious; so we told him that he could be in the book if he wrote eulogies of us; which he did. But his tongue was not where it should have been.

Meanwhile we were going to the very serious meetings of the Fugitive group—too serious we thought, hence the dedicatory page of *The Golden Mean*—and we, the young ones, were trying all kinds of poetry, from Edna Millay to Eliot, from Robinson to Cummings, who had just appeared. All things were possible in that time to us all, the older and the younger men alike.

The quickening of the imagination in the South twenty-five years ago seems to be an acknowledged fact. I believe it was a little different from the literary excitement in other regions at that time. After the war the South again knew the world, but it had a memory of another war. With us, entering the world once more meant not the obliteration of the past but a heightened consciousness of it; so that we had, at any rate in Nashville, a double focus, a looking two ways, which gave a special dimension to the writings of our school—not necessarily a superior quality—which American writing as a whole seemed to lack.

Not at that time, not in fact until about 1927, did we become consciously historical and sectional; yet we were all from that region—Ransom, Davidson, the two Willses, Warren, Moore, and I all being either Tennesseans or Kentuckians; I was born the farthest away, the Kentucky Blue Grass. Nobody ever did anything to bring this group together; the university did not "encourage writers"; none of us went there to become writers. We simply went there. And there we were. The great universities of the East could have boasted in that period groups of writers quite as good as ours, or better, though I doubt it; yet they were not groups in our sense, being associated only through the university and having a cosmopolitan range of interest without, I think, a simple homogeneous background which they could take with them to the university where it might suffer little or no break in continuity.

I would call the Fugitives an intensive and historical group as opposed to the eclectic and cosmopolitan groups that flourished in the East. There was a sort of unity of feeling, of which we were not then very much aware, which came out of—to give it a big name—a common historical myth; and its use for the dramatic and lyrical arts, I believe, is that it expresses itself in the simple ritual of greeting a friend in the street. Although we disagreed, and at times quarreled, we had, in addition to the peculiar solidarity of artists everywhere, a deep understanding that gave even the quarrels a special intensity and form. Given this sort of group, I think I may disregard the claims of propriety and say quite plainly that, so far as I know, there was never so much talent, knowledge, and character accidentally brought together in one American place in our time.

I left Nashville late in 1923. In the next four years, which include two years after *The Fugitive* ceased publication, I was in New York, but I tried to keep up with the old group: we were constantly sending our poems back and forth. And then one day—I cannot be sure of the year, I think 1926—I wrote John Ransom a new sort of letter. I told him that we must do something about Southern history and the culture of the South. John had written, on the same day, the same message to me. The letters crossed in the mail. Out of this new interest came *I'll Take My Stand* and new writers, not poets but historians, novelists, and economists, who are altogether another story. To Donald Davidson more than to any other man belongs the later phase; but that is his story, not mine.

The Gaze Past,
The Glance Present
Forty Years After
The Fugitive
1962

DONALD DAVIDSON has probably written more poems than any other member of the old Fugitive group except Robert Penn Warren. In this new volume (*The Long Street*, Vanderbilt University Press, 1962), which I assume contains all the poems he wants to keep after more than forty years of writing, he offers us, from 1919 to the present, only thirty-five pieces. Of these, eleven, or almost a third, go back to the twenties; yet the early poems are short and the bulk of the work is later and, I think, more impressive than anything that Davidson wrote before 1930 except "Lee in the Mountains," a great elegiac monologue which inexplicably is not included in this book.* But it is the early work by which Donald Davidson is chiefly known: not only known but "placed," by people who have not read him, as a regional poet of nostalgia for the Old South. In the general observations that follow I wish to pay homage to an American poet of perfect independence and integrity, and in a shorter view to correct (insofar as it is possible to correct indifference)

---

*When writing this article, I mistakenly assumed that *The Long Street* would be a "Selected Poems"; hence my complaint that "Lee in the Mountains" and some other poems were not included here.

the belief that Davidson wants to "restore" the Old South
and would be willing to undertake extreme "reactionary"
measures to bring the restoration about. The poetry, in this
view, is a kind of sublimated frustration.

What Mr. Davidson may want to restore, or not restore,
or to destroy or create, is not the issue raised by a reading
of these poems. What, in his poems, he is concerned with is
the opposition of an heroic myth to the secularization of man
in our age. Looked at from this point of view, his poetry is
no more concerned with the restoration of the Old South
than the *Aeneid* is with the restoration of Troy, or Aeschylus
with bringing back to life Mycenae after the destruction of
the House of Atreus. His later poems consciously reaffirm the
continuity of a quasi-religious myth, composed of classical
and Christian elements.

The question that Mr. Davidson's myth suggests is not
whether it is "true"; it can no more be proved than the myth
of Democratic Man, under which we live at present. All myths
seem to allow for their own disintegration. I must make this
matter personal, and ask myself how much of my own myth,
insofar as I am conscious of having one, I can see in Davidson's. I can see much of my myth, though I should like to
see, if not all of it, then a great deal more. There is not one
poem in the book to which I cannot give entire assent; I
should merely like to see more to assent to. These poems say
something important about man in our time, even though
they may be about a country fiddler or Mr. Davidson's pa-
tronymic ancestor, or about the mystery of time and motion
in "At the Station." The gaze is into the past but the glance
is at the present, and this glance is sharp and exact.

The region that Mr. Davidson occupies, and that I do not
see myself in, is one in which historical relativity seems to
have little play. It is not that I don't agree with my old friend
Don about what is wrong with the modern world; it is rather
that I don't agree when he says, elusively yet unmistakably,
that if the South had won, it would all have been not only

different but better. (One is reminded of T. S. Eliot's remark about Ezra Pound, that for Mr. Pound hell is for those "other people"; and one infers that, but for *them*, etc., etc.) Mr. Davidson long ago put his faith in history, and history in 1865 grievously let him down. Well, it let a lot of other people, including myself, down too, insofar as I can imagine 1865; but this, for me, is not the main consideration. My relativism —historical only, not philosophical and moral—tells me that the heroic South could not have lasted, and that a Southern victory might have hastened its disappearance. For the Confederacy to have survived, the development of competitive power would have followed military victory and political independence. I surmise that the neo-Greek political philosophers of South Carolina would have been as eager as the next one to enter the international power race. So I am convinced —if one can be convinced of what didn't happen—that a uniform industrial civilization would have spread over the "two countries"; so that the South today would be even more "Yankee" than it actually is. One must entertain the paradox that the South has enjoyed a longer period of identity in defeat than it might have been able to preserve in victory.

I trust that persons who may have been patient enough to read this will not conclude that I agree with the fatuous Southerners who are now enthusiastically collaborating in the centennial celebrations of the South's defeat. It is not "good" that the South was defeated; only fools can rejoice in defeat. I have merely tried in this article to imagine what *might* be had the South won; and that is a different matter altogether.

In any case I do not see how it would have been possible for Donald Davidson's South to survive in any historical circumstance imaginable at present. A Southern victory, I repeat, might have done more than defeat to destroy his simple, patriarchal — and, mind you, slaveless — society; for Mr. Davidson's Old South has always seemed to me to leave about half of the Old South out of the account: the half, or third, or whatever the figures were, that included the Negro.

I have said little about the poems themselves. Although Mr. Davidson has taught English all his mature life, he is one of the best classical scholars I know; not a philologist, but a lover of *literae humaniores*. His lifelong reading of the Latin and Greek classics is more and more reflected in the simplicity and elegance of his diction, and in the unobtrusive formalism of his versification. *The Long Street* is one of the most impressive collections of American poetry since the first World War. It is all the more remarkable for its appearance late in Donald Davidson's career. To bring one's affection and admiration together, so that these emotions, rare even in isolation, are indistinguishable, is a privilege enjoyed not more than three or four times in one's life.

Reflections on the
Death of John Crowe Ransom

1974

JOHN CROWE RANSOM died on July 3, fifty-four years after the first issue of *The Fugitive* appeared. Donald Davidson died in 1968. Robert Penn Warren and I are left of the men who became poet-critics and whose lives were powerfully influenced by J. C. R. I would say, with Yeats, that I am accustomed to his lack of breath, but it will be harder to believe that he no longer occupies space, silent and unknowing as he was in the last few years. Now we may ignore, as we see fit, the destructive revisions which this great elegiac poet inflicted upon many of his finest poems.

I wrote and gave as a speech at Kenyon College a eulogy of John on his eightieth birthday. I hope the reader will understand it when I say that I didn't like him while I was his student. That was more than fifty years ago. I thought him cold, calculating, and highly competitive. I can say this because I, too, was calculating and competitive, and I was arrogant enough as his student, and even later, until about 1930, to think I was a rival! But I was not, like him, cold: I was *calidus juventa*, running over with violent feelings, usually directed at my terrible family—terrible because my father had humiliated us; and now that I was in college there was not enough money to see me through. (My brother Ben said many years later that we were brought up with silver spoons in our mouths and were expected to eat the spoons.) My dislike of John was my fear of him. He had perfect self-control; I could see him flush with anger, but his language was always moderate and urbane. I was just the opposite, and some of my dislike came of my exposure to his critical glance. His patience with my irregular behavior only made his disapproval the more telling. What disturbed and challenged me most was my sense of the logical propriety of his attitude towards his students. He never rebuked us; his subtle withdrawal of attention was more powerful than reproach: he refused to be overtly aware of our lapses.

Logic was the mode of his thought and sensibility. It limited his criticism to a kind of neo-classicism, but it contained, as "structure," his poetry; and thus the defect of the one became the virtue of the other. I have for years wondered how such an acute intelligence could seriously consider any formula for poetry, and I am still amazed that John Ransom, of all people, could come up with "structure" and "texture" as critical metaphors. After the elaborate essays in Kantian philosophical aesthetics, the simple structure-texture formula is a sad anticlimax—as sad as the late Yvor Winters' formula. Winters said, over some thirty years, that "the concept motivates the emotion." I can't pause here for a discussion of these two famous prescriptive shortcuts to the meaning of poetry; and I shall merely indicate their similarity to a somewhat less famous formula that the single word "tension" conceals. It is not, of course, tension in the ordinary sense, though certain poems may be described as "*in*tense." What the inventor of poetic "tension" had in mind was a pseudo-erudite pun; that is, he dropped the prefixes of the logical terms *extension* and *intension*, and had tension derived from both, and containing both. Intension is connotation, or Ransom's structure, provided, of course, that the objects denoted are in an acceptable syntactical relation. May we say that Winters' concept is Ransom's structure, and his emotion, Ransom's texture? All these correspondences are only proximate, but they witness a remarkably similar critical impulse in men of different ages and backgrounds. I have no explanation of the astonishing fact that three Americans but no Europeans in the modern age tried to encapsulate poetry.

In the summer of 1923 John Ransom wrote an essay entitled "Waste Lands" and published it in the *Literary Review* of the *New York Evening Post* (later the independent *Saturday Review*). He attacked T. S. Eliot for the obvious reasons, such as fragmentary prosody and expository discontinuity or, as he would have later described it, lack of structure. I saw the attack as the result of his irritation with my praise of Eliot, which was that of a distant disciple, to the neglect of him, my actual master from whom I learned more than I could even now describe and acknowledge. I wrote an impertinent—no, an insolent—reply to the essay; John answered me; and I should have been flattered but was "hurt" instead. That is why I "disliked" him. I had already learned from Eliot too, but I had used him, in our "Fugitive" meetings, for my egotistical assertion of superiority over my benighted friends. Who else in Tennessee had discovered Eliot? Who else had read Remy de Gourmont, Gerard de Nerval, and Charles Baudelaire? I was even vain about my Greek, which was quite elementary; John Ransom could have humiliated me with his professional mastery which he had acquired under Herbert Cushing Tolman (also my revered teacher) and then at Christ Church, Oxford. When I said in a previous chapter of this book that John Ransom and Donald Davidson were everything to me, I meant and still mean it. My "dislike" of John, I repeat, was my fear of him.

After I went to New York in 1924 he sent me his new poems and tried out some of his ideas with me—the ideas that led to the writing of his remarkable *God Without Thunder*. (This book later gave me certain philosophical terms that enabled me to write my contribution to *I'll Take My Stand*.) John later repudiated the liturgical Christianity advocated in *God Without Thunder*. I still agree with the main argument of that book; that is, I don't see how Christianity can survive as a humanistic doctrine: there must be a theistic God, apodeictic and menacing as well as merciful. Almost twenty-five years later John wrote, in *The New Republic*, a review of Eliot's *Collected Poems*, in which it appears that religion is for persons who are suffering from a sense of sin, but poetry comes from, and to, those lucky people who are capable of simple delight in nature. That was John's polite way of putting Eliot in his place thirty years after his rougher handling of that inconvenient "lion in the path." And ten years later still, he wrote a "handsome" (one of John's favorite adjectives in a similar context)—a very handsome analytical tribute to "Gerontion" for the Eliot memorial volume which I edited the year after Eliot's death. The actions of this logical man were unpredictable.

And he was a great man—he has been near me daily since his death two months ago—who carried on his back, not time's wallet, but an intolerable burden of conflict that only occasionally, and even then indirectly, came to the surface. His reply to my attack on his "Waste Lands" seemed to discredit me as a callow youth in revolt against his teacher; I was that, of course, but his rebuttal was, more deeply, an indirect assertion of his authoritative role at Vanderbilt University: for a recent student to question that authority menaced his position. The polemic was deeper than logic. His logic justified his anger.

During the years 1922-1925 of *The Fugitive*, John's restraint must have been sorely tried many times. He was the only mature poet in the group. His immature *Poems About God* was several years behind him, and he was writing some of the great poems which were published in *Chills and Fever* in 1924. John Ransom was not an innovator in the sense that both Pound and Eliot were. He was a sly, subtle innovator in ways that could not be imitated and could not found a school. He wrote in conventional stanzas and meters, but his sensibility owed nothing to any poet, past or present. (Some critics have seen in him Hardy, others Donne. But this means little. Every poet resembles some other poet somewhere; if he didn't he would be an idiot.) Most of the great poems— "The Equilibrists," "Bells for John Whiteside's Daughter," "Vaunting Oak," "Spectral Lovers," "Winter Remembered," "Necrological," "Captain Carpenter"—all these in *Chills and Fever*—were written between 1922 and 1924. After 1924 his work lay in another direction: critical and philosophical prose. But in the thirties he wrote two of his finest—in my opinion, his greatest—poems: "Painted Head" and "Prelude to an Evening." The latter he ruined by rewriting it so that it would have a "happy ending." Nevertheless, the original version cannot be destroyed. I infer that "Painted Head" pleased him in his old age: until his literary executor finds a revised version among his papers, we may believe the poem is safe.

In the past ten years I have thought of John's mania (I don't know what else to call it) as the last infirmity of a truly noble mind. Yet one must see his compulsive revisions as a quite consistent activity, as an extension of his reliance on *logic* as the ultimate standard of judgment. Consider his repudiation of Agrarianism in 1945, in an essay "Art and the Human Economy." He sent me the typescript before he published it in *The Kenyon Review*. He dismissed Agrarianism as sentimental and nostalgic, lacking in the sense of the immediate American reality. I urged him to suppress the essay, on the ground that when one finds a new interest, one need not repudiate an old one: one simply moves on. He published it, and lost the friendship of his old friend Donald Davidson. But never mind—John was only being logically consistent! And, of course, one finds the same logic back of the notorious

essay "Shakespeare at Sonnets." John had been reading
Donne, and had derived a formula for "metaphysical" poetry
that raised Donne above Shakespeare the sonneteer. This
formula was strictly logical, giving a poem by Donne a coherent center that a Shakespeare sonnet lacked. The editors,
Brooks and Warren, of *The Southern Review*, felt that they
had to publish the essay, but only after futile efforts to get
John to suppress it or at least to tone it down.

It appeared in 1938, and it attracted more attention than
any other essay that John had written up to that time. His
great essays—either written with his logical guard down, or
perhaps the subjects bypassed it—are "Poets Without
Laurels" and "Wanted: An Ontological Critic." The ontological critic would investigate the grades of reality that a
poem embodied. What other critic, almost an exact contemporary of John's, had arrived at the same doctrine though in
very different terms? What other critic had also studied philosophy with the intention of teaching it or of becoming in
some other capacity a professional philosopher? The one guess
as to the answer is: T. S. Eliot. (Neither liked the other's
criticism. Eliot liked Ransom's poetry better than Ransom
liked his. Eliot's opinions I got by word of mouth; Ransom's,
by word of mouth and from published essays and reviews.)
The doctrine they shared is an ancient one that every age
must rediscover. Eliot: whether a work is poetry must be
decided by literary criteria; whether it is *great* poetry, by
other than literary criteria. Ransom: the grade of being, or
the ontological value, of a poem, must be discerned philosophically by critics of sufficient wisdom; whether the work is
poetry will depend on its degree of rightness in the structure-
texture relation, neither obscuring the other. What both Eliot
and Ransom arrive at in the end is that only persons ripe
in experience both of literature and of the world can be proper
critics of poetry.

Ransom's other great essay, "Poets Without Laurels," I
consider the *locus classicus* for insight into the relation of the

modern poet to industrial-technological society. The poet is no longer a public figure; he is no longer "laureled." He is a private person who writes poems for other poets to read. He writes pure poetry (Stevens) or obscure poetry (Tate!). All this is commonplace? The simple truth is never commonplace unless it is spoken by a commonplace mind. I risk the guess that Eliot's essays will be read, by that mythical character posterity, for their opinions; Ransom's, for their style, regardless of what they say. For John Ransom wrote the most perspicuous, the most engaging, and the most elegant prose of all the poet-critics of our time.

A few days after his death I came across (for at least the hundredth time) an essay entitled "In Amicitia." He wrote it for my sixtieth birthday. This essay isolates me; for surely I am the only pupil who has ever had such affectionate approbation from his master. For John Crowe Ransom was Vergil to me, his apprentice. It is proper to recall the words of another apprentice:

I salute thee, Montovano. . . .

Miss Toklas' American Cake
1971

THAT DAY in Oxford was foggy and cold, but we were ready to leave. I went on ahead with the luggage to Newhaven where early the next morning we were to take the channel boat to Dieppe—the longest but cheapest crossing to France. We took passage but I remember little about it—nothing until we arrived at the Gare du Nord and were shoved into a taxi by a porter whose *argot* I couldn't understand. I remember shouting to the taxi driver "Numero seese, rue de Fleurus" over and over again, while he looked at me with disdain; but at last he smiled and said, "Numero seese, rue de Fleur*s*," enunciating the "s" which in my reading-French I thought as a terminal consonant was silent. Then, with a smile, "Rive gauche"; and I was blank and bewildered. I thought he was saying that Fleurus Street was a left-handed or even an awkward dream.

After about twenty minutes of hazardous driving, which took us through the dank and drizzly grandeurs of the Place de la Concorde, we arrived at the Hôtel de Fleurus, where there were reservations for my wife, myself, our three-year-old daughter, and for Miss Léonie Adams, who had been with us in Oxford, and who had now accompanied us to France. We were huddled into the creaking *ascenseur* and taken to the *première étage*, or second floor, to a room looking down upon a grey and featureless street. The reservations had been made by Ford Madox Ford who had taken me under his wing in New York the year before. A few minutes after we were installed in our *belle chambre* the *femme de charge* appeared at the door and handed me two sealed envelopes—"Pour monsieur et madame." One note was from Ford, welcoming us to Paris and explaining how to get to his flat at 32 rue de Vaugirard, a pleasant walk of about ten minutes around the Luxembourg Gardens. The other message was portentous; it read:

You and your wife will come to tea on
Thursday at 27 rue de Fleurus. *Gertrude Stein.*

I didn't know the hour of tea in Paris, but no doubt Ford would enlighten us, which he did the next day when we dined with him in his fourth-floor flat. I showed him Miss Stein's command and expressed some surprise at the "You will come"; but Ford brushed aside my "I'll be damned if I will" with: "Never mind—Gertrude is a great lady." I was so provincial that I wondered then and later if American women in Paris could become great ladies without first being ladies. We—my wife, Léonie, and I—went to Miss Stein's Thursday, the first of many Thursdays that winter; for, once admitted to the *salon*, one was expected to appear with some regularity. It was almost as if Professor Stein were calling the roll and absences were noted with a black mark somewhere in the recesses of her computer memory.

The *mise en scène* of the famous flat at 27 rue de Fleurus I shall describe later. Meanwhile I must say something about my continuing education, which had been deficient at college, and partly frustrated by four years of free-lance reviewing in New York. Now I was in Europe, in 1928, on a Guggenheim

Fellowship. Miss Adams and I were the second and third poets to enjoy the Guggenheim patronage, Countee Cullen having been the first. Here I was to have leisure for the first time in the six years since my graduation from Vanderbilt —and here through the "Tate Luck" (Robert Penn Warren's not unkindly but not very precise generalization about his friend) I was about to plunge into the French experience which young literary Americans in the twenties thought they must have or remain sorry provincials.

The Guggenheim stipend was enough for sustenance but not enough for the luxury of the grand tour, and only enough for an infrequent *apéritif* at the Ritz Bar, where everybody knew that Scott and Zelda appeared every afternoon, when in Paris, to reassure Scott's admirers that he was still making $30,000 a year. The Fitzgeralds were not there that autumn of 1928, nor was Ernest Hemingway, but they were there the next autumn as I shall in due time relate. These men had something to do with my continuing education but not until ten months later.

My European education, which the Guggenheim Foundation insisted upon since one could not get the stipend if one stayed at home, was largely in the English language of a *petit cercle*. I met in my first year in France very few French people, writers or mere citizens; and this seemed to be true of most of the Americans in Paris. However, in the two months in England preceding that dark journey across the channel I had met many English writers, some of whom became lifetime friends: F. S. Flint, L. A. G. Strong, Harold Monro, Richard Church, Herbert Read, F. V. Morley (half American), and T. S. Eliot.

Early in 1929 Ford left for America and turned his flat over to us. This *homme de lettres*, who had been a great editor and was now the greatest living British novelist, lived in Spartan frugality. His flat consisted of a *petit salon* furnished with a divan which, like that of the typist in "The Waste Land," became at night a bed; this room, in the

British phrase, was the bed-sitting-room of my wife and me. At the far end was a small room with a small bed occupied by our daughter; near the entrance a narrow closet was just large enough for Miss Adams. The dining space is now dim in my memory; and there must have been a bathroom, or what passed for one in a *petit bourgeois* flat—a drain without a seat, requiring considerable acrobatic agility, and referred to by John Bishop, when he came to see me, as "pre-germ-theory French plumbing."

Also on that *troisième étage*, around a bend in the hall, there was another flat of several small rooms occupied by Stella Bowen, Ford's common-law wife (necessarily common-law because Ford never succeeded in getting an English divorce from his first wife, Elsie Martindale), and his daughter Julie by Stella. Julie was three years older than my daughter Nancy, and in the course of that winter she taught Nancy to speak French and forget her English. We could not be certain that Ford and Stella were separated. This uncertainty was another step forward in my European education. It was Stella, a brilliant portrait painter, who a year later introduced me to Ezra Pound and Edith Sitwell—the former a distant literary hero, the latter somewhat later a lifelong friend.

I had been given the Guggenheim grant to write verse and to broaden my mind through conversation with French writers. After January 1929 I wrote a few poems, but the work I did every morning in Ford's flat might have been better done in New York, or Richmond, or Nashville. For I was slugging away at a popular, or what I hoped would be a popular, life of Jefferson Davis to follow up the small success of a similar book about Thomas J. Jackson, which I had written in order to persuade my publisher to issue my first book of verse, *Mr. Pope and Other Poems*. This book had come out in New York shortly before we sailed for England. The few Jefferson Davis reference books available were in the American Library, which was presided over by Mr. Burton

E. Stevenson, of *The Home Book of Verse* fame, who was
as perplexed as I was that I should be writing in Paris about
the Confederate president. One day he asked me to come to
his office, and there introduced me to a Mr. Slidell. This
elderly gentleman was the son of the Confederate ambassador
to the court of Napoleon III. His English was Oxonian and
his attire that of a Frenchman of about 1890. He was an
American citizen who had been in America only the four
years he spent at Princeton. At a later meeting, by appoint-
ment at the Café de Dumesnil, I found him charming but
ignorant of Confederate history and a little bored by my
interest in it.

Could Mr. Slidell have been a part of my education as a
modern poet? I daresay no one knows what a poet's education
should be; John Milton seems to have calculated every step;
but a modern poet must take what comes, both persons and
books. Along with *The Official Records of the Union and
Confederate Armies*, of which the American Library had a
complete set in fifty-two volumes, I read Bergson, of whom
I had not heard at Vanderbilt, Péguy, Léon Bloy, François
Mauriac, and in my halting Italian (more halting than my
French) the *Breviario di estetica* of Benedetto Croce. I also
read odds and ends of living French poets: for the first time,
the great poems of Paul Valéry and the early poems, such
as "Crusoé" and "Anabase," of St.-John Perse, who fifteen
years later in Washington became my good friend. Was this
reading—and more, such as *Swann's Way* and the early novels
of Francis Carco—was all this reading a part of my continuing education?

Observation of men and manners must have been equally,
if intangibly, contributive. There was Colonel Charles
Sweeney, whom I don't remember how I met, a foreign cor-
respondent for a New York paper, who had been an officer
of the Foreign Legion and later a colonel in the French
Army, a friend of Ernest Hemingway who told me about him
almost a year before I knew him. I shall not forget one thing

he said about Hemingway—that although from Oak Park, Illinois, Ernest was a Mediterranean type, extroverted, suspicious, unloyal, and violent. (I last ran into Charlie Sweeney in Salt Lake City twenty years later where he was living out his decline at the villa of a Mrs. Allen, heiress of a copper fortune, and too feeble to go hunting with his friend Hem, to whom he made occasional visits in Idaho.) With Charlie Sweeney one talked about war, safaris, the rise of Hitler, women—the "usual subjects of conversation," in Pound's words in the *Cantos*, "between intelligent men."

But with Valéry Larbaud and Julien Green the conversation was quite different: it was intellectual French *haute bourgeoisie*. Larbaud was not a great writer but a first-rate literary intelligence such as only France produced in that era. I was introduced to him by Sylvia Beach at tea in her famous bookshop at 12 rue de l'Odéon, and he was at once kind to me. He invited me to come to his flat for a late afternoon *apéritif* to see his armies of lead soldiers. In a large loft-like room there was a long table, about 20′ by 10′, covered with brown sand, arranged in valleys and hills, with clumps of small trees stuck here and there. There were hundreds of lead soldiers formed in line or their backs turned in flight. This, he explained, was the Battle of Borodino, and he pointed out the figure of Napoleon overlooking the battle from a low hillock, and some ten feet away at the far end of the terrain, Kutuzov, sitting on a stump, his back turned to the line of battle. Larbaud explained, rather apologetically, that he didn't have enough Union and Confederate soldiers to fight the Battle of Gettysburg, but he could set up the skirmish at which the gallant Pelham was killed; and he showed me beautifully executed figures of General Grant smoking a cigar, General Lee mounted augustly on Traveller, and, surprisingly, General Leonidas Polk, the fighting Bishop; one of the founders of the University of the South, where forty years later I went to live. On one of my three or four visits to his flat he gave me a copy of his *Fauteuil XXXVIII,*

an introduction to the poetry of Valéry. Although neither
then or later could I fully understand this difficult poet,
Larbaud's book was a great help; and later when I told
Edmund Wilson about it, he got the dates mixed and wrote
somewhere that my "Ode to the Confederate Dead" had been
influenced by "Le Cimetière Marin." I wrote my poem in
1926; I first read Valèry in 1928.

I have not known anybody before or since like Julien
Green, the shyest young man I have ever met. Perhaps
Larbaud or Paul Morand, whom I had met a few times at
the flat of Adrienne Monnier, told him about a young American from the South who was an apprentice poet and who
had written about Confederate heroes. Green's family was
Southern, from Fauquier County, Virginia, and he had been
for a while at the University of Virginia. He asked me to meet
him one afternoon at the Café des Deux Magots to arrange
a visit to Paul Valéry. (A few days afterwards, a conflict
interfered, and I never met Valéry.) Julien seemed to me
completely French, and he assumed that my French was as
good as his; but I soon lapsed into English, which he spoke
more elegantly than I did. What was Southern about him
was then immediately apparent. Whom did I know? Whom
was I kin to? He had been in Charlottesville in the summer
of 1919; I too was there that summer taking a course in New
Testament Greek. We did our reading in adjoining cubicles
in the old Rotunda, then the library, and looked out at the
same giant magnolia which was in full bloom. But we didn't
meet. This reminiscence almost ten years later was our
Southern bond. When we met at the Deux Magots, I had
just read *Léviathan*, which I still think is one of the great
modern novels. After 1928 I didn't see Julien Green again
until 1941, when he came to see me with Denis de Rougemont
in Princeton. By that time he had reconverted to Catholicism
and was a devout communicant. Jacques Maritain told me
that the conversion came as a result of Julien's suddenly beginning to chant from memory long passages from the *Psalms*.

If Miss Stein had her Thursdays, Ford had his Saturday evenings four flights up at 32 rue de Vaugirard. This was still the late autumn, or early December, of 1928, before Ford turned the flat over to us and went to New York. The faithful were Léonie, Caroline, and I, and two other literati who attended at intervals. There was a man who had a hole in his head, an avant-garde poet named Lincoln Gillespie; the hole was covered by a silver plate. "You don't believe me?" he would say; and he always said it, forgetting that he had told us before. He would lean forward, push back a strand of hair, and ask me to tap the plate.

Gillespie had contributed to *transition*, a famous avant-garde journal edited by a trilingual man named Eugène Jolas. I had had things in it too; but why I was eligible for publication in an avant-garde magazine I never knew. Gene Jolas was married to a fine American girl named Nancy McDonald, from Henderson, Kentucky, a near cousin of a fraternity brother of mine at Vanderbilt; but she was not interested in Kentucky and charmingly snubbed my naively provincial manners. Jolas was a dedicated man, convinced that literature would soon lose its national roots; and he issued in *transition* a manifesto called "The Revolution of the Word," which about thirty French and American writers signed, but which Hart Crane and I and, I believe, John Bishop, Hemingway, and Fitzgerald refused to sign. "The Revolution of the Word" was largely based upon Joyce's "Work in Progress," which, when completed, became *Finnegans Wake*. (Poor Jolas' "Revolution of the Word," at the distance of forty years, looks more and more like "Deterioration of the Word.")

The other remarkable attendant at Ford's Saturdays was, like Mr. Slidell, a survivor of the pre-war period, a formalist poet who wrote at least one memorable poem in *terza rima*, about an "insulted soul" who had lingered late in the Luxembourg and found himself locked in overnight. Mr. Dunning —I never took a liberty with him—Mr. Dunning wore neatly threadbare striped trousers, a wing collar, a cravat (not a necktie), and carried a clouded stick. He lived in two rooms in the courtyard of 72-bis rue Notre Dame des Champs, where we occasionally went to tea. Pound had turned the flat over to him when he left Paris for Rapallo. His tea was a different leaf from that of Miss Stein's—brewed very black and given us without either sugar or milk. Hemingway later told me that Dunning, having kicked hashish and heroin, would boil a pound of tea in a pint of water and go off for two days on what is now called a "trip." Mr. Dunning's manners were perfect. He was shyly attentive to Léonie, who was equally shy but remote. Thirty years later, long after his death, Ralph Cheever Dunning was the subject of one of the few sympathetic portraits in Hemingway's *A Moveable Feast*. That book, you will remember, ends at 1926; I am glad that I didn't meet Ernest Hemingway until September 1929.

Ford taught us all the art of the fictional time-shift; so I shall now use it to jump ahead a year and finish off the *récit* of Ford's Saturday evenings. In 1928 they were *soirées*, during which we sat at the feet of the master; Ford, however, talked little but rather nodded agreement or disagreement. Occasionally he might glance backwards at his early life: "My great-great-grandfather in Poland repudiated his titles and moved to Alsace." We shall never know whether that was true; it could have been. But in the autumn of 1929 the *soirées* became much more literary and tyrannously competitive. We were commanded to play a difficult French parlor game called *bouts-rimés*. Ford passed around pencils and paper and assigned us the rhyme words of a Shakespeare sonnet or of a sonnet by "my aunt Christina Rossetti, a beautiful poet." Everybody had to use the assigned rhymes, and the winning sonnet was graded on both its quality and the speed of its composition. Ford himself usually won and gave as a second prize a melancholy-looking round cake which was sliced at once and eaten with moderate zest by the company.

I can't remember whether Mr. Dunning came in 1929. Mr. Gillespie was still at hand. A remarkable young man, Howard Baker from California, a *protégé* of Yvor Winters, joined the *petit cercle*. Howard wrote some excellent poetry; a fine poem may still be read—his other verse is not in print —in the *Oxford Book of American Verse*. After Paris he taught for a while at Harvard; then he married the lady who wrote *Young Man with a Horn* and retired to an orange grove in California, whence he infrequently sends out a brilliant essay on classical literature.

Now, back in early 1929, in Ford's flat, I sat every morning at a small table typing away at my Jefferson Davis, as oblivious of France as if I had been in Montgomery, Alabama, in 1861, to report the organization of the Confederate Government. So, from January to July of that year, the passing time was and still is a little vague, except that I saw a great deal of my dear friend John Peale Bishop, of whom I shall presently have more to say.

All that winter and well into the spring I went two or three times a week to the American Library to check dates, hours, persons, and places in the 1860s and not less frequently than once a week I saw Miss Alice B. Toklas either enter or leave, carrying a large reticule stuffed with books. We passed the time of day, but I was never sure, in my speaking acquaintance with her of almost a year, that she knew my name. I remember asking the lady at the library desk whether Miss Toklas could read all those books in a week. No, the librarian said, Miss Toklas was a cultivated lady and must certainly read better books. The books in the reticule were invariably stories of the Northwest Mounted Police, or westerns of the genre of Zane Grey, and they were for Miss Stein, who, she had been told, seldom read anything else. The favorite student of William James and Hugo Münsterberg had evidently, as a psychologist, passed beyond literature, and felt an aversion from it, along with a dislike of the United States. Bernard Fay, a portly Frenchman who had written a life of Benjamin

Franklin and who was always at the Thursdays, told me that
he had learned more about America from Gertrude than from
all the books he had read. Her key to America was the five-
and-ten-cent store, the New York subway, and the baseball
stories of Ring Lardner. He didn't include James Oliver Curwood and Miss Toklas' reticule, so I inferred that Miss Stein's
reading was her own affair. I had read her *Three Lives* and
had admired the story "Melanctha"; I wondered why she
had given up straight English. Hemingway told me that
Gertrude was too vain and too lazy to compete with other
writers, and had invented her own style, for which there were
no standards of judgment, and nothing with which to com-
pare it.

I wrote the last page of my Jefferson Davis on Bastille
Day. Late that evening I joined my wife and some assorted
compatriots at the apartment of William Aspenwall Bradley,
a literary agent and the translator of some of the works of
Remy de Gourmont. We saw from his high front windows
facing the Seine, with Notre Dame in the middle distance, the
spectacular display of fireworks celebrating the hundred and
fortieth anniversary of the fall of the Bastille. The next day
we—my wife and daughter and Miss Adams—set out for
Brittany where we spent the summer at Concarneau. Miss
Adams stayed at a small *pension* some distance down the
beach from our hostel, Le Grand Hôtel des Cornouailles. A
fellow guest at her *pension* was a young man named Leon
Edel, the future distinguished biographer of Henry James,
who told Miss Adams that he had seen in the New York
Nation the list of the new Guggenheim Fellows and was glad
to see the names of two Negro writers, Countee Cullen and
Allen Tate. Miss Adams brought Mr. Edel to meet us the
next day, and I felt that he was uneasy and disconcerted.
When we became good friends—I still see him often in New
York—he told me that at Concarneau, at our first meeting,
he thought for a moment that I was an albino black who was
trying to "pass."

After a chilly summer on a rough beach where the sea was cold, the food at the Grand Hôtel greasy, and only the blue, red, and green sails of the sardine boats lent color, we returned in September to Paris and went at once to the Hôtel de la Place de l'Odéon. Ford was back from New York and an unsuccessful courtship of a lady from St. Louis, for which he had spent almost the last farthing of the large sums he had made from *Some Do Not, A Man Could Stand Up,* and *No More Parades.* He was again in the flat at 32 rue de Vaugirard and was about to resume his Saturdays, only this time, as I have related, with *bouts-rimés* as the attraction, to say nothing of the round, stale, iced cake. Two new recruits at the Saturdays whom I forgot a moment ago were a Dr. McCarthy, a small, mincing fellow, always dressed in sombre black suits and stiff high collars, who took short steps in patent leather shoes topped by grey spats. He was later reputed to have been the prototype of the famous transvestite doctor in Djuna Barnes' *Nightwood.* Of Djuna herself I saw little—she had her own closed circle—and little of Hart Crane, who was in Paris in 1929; but they are both another story. The other recruit at the *bouts-rimés* was the Canadian novelist Morley Callaghan, not• a regular attendant, and somewhat derisive of the entertainment, who seemed not to understand that we too were bored but that we were there because we respected and loved the Master, who was disinterestedly kind to those who disliked him, as well as to those who loved him. (I never heard Ford speak ill of any writer but H. G. Wells, who, he said, flattered him privately and denigrated him publicly.)

In the autumn of 1929 I spent two or three evenings a week playing dominoes or Russian Bank with Ford at the Deux Magots or the Closerie des Lilas; he needed at least four cognacs every night to prevent insomnia. One evening, walking back from the Closerie des Lilas by the Petit Luxembourg, he said, as if talking to himself: "One would like either to have been an English milord or have a chair in the Académie

Française." By this time he was hated in England, had been
dropped by fair-weather friends in New York, and was admired only in France. His pathos was that he was not completely English, could not be American, and although almost
wholly French in culture and sensibility could not be one of
the French immortals. At about this same time I was told
by William Bird (who had first published Hemingway) or by
William Aspenwall Bradley—I remember talking about the
book with both Bird and Bradley—that Gallimard had asked
Ford to suggest a translator for *The Good Soldier*, and that
Ford told Gallimard he knew a good translator whom he
could get to do the job without pay. Three months later Ford
brought Gallimard the translation, which he himself had done,
by simply rewriting the book in French without looking at
the English. I once compared about fifty pages of the English
and the French, sentence by sentence; the correspondence
was minutely exact. Years later I asked Ford why he had
not made it easier for himself by following the English text;
he replied that that would have got him into thinking in
English and ruined the French idioms. He said then that he
had had the entire novel—every sentence—in his head before
be began to write it in 1913. He had the most prodigious
memory I have encountered in any man. And *The Good
Soldier* is not only his masterpiece, but in my view the masterpiece of British fiction in this century.

Early in September, not only were we in Paris again, but
Miss Stein and Miss Toklas were back at 27 rue de Fleurus
from their summer in the Midi, and I was asked with some
other people to drop by for tea, although it was not Thursday.
She said to me, "Tate"—I was always Tate and she Miss
Stein, for an obscure inhibition stopped Gertrude at my
epiglottis—"Tate," she said, "it's too bad you've stopped
writing poetry." (I thought I had scarcely begun.) She
pointed to a thick stack of typewriter paper, possibly two
hundred sheets, and said: "A few poems I wrote this summer." I envied her fluency—or would it be fluidity? Not long

after this incident I strolled through the Luxembourg early
one evening. After seeing Ford to the door at 32, and hearing
the shrewish concierge answer his "Cordon, s'il vous plait,"
I walked around the Musée de Luxembourg and saw approach-
ing a familiar rotund figure with a large white dog on a long
leash. It was Miss Stein giving Basket, her poodle, his exercise
before bedtime. I said something like "Good evening, Miss
Stein—this is Allen Tate." She stopped and a faint smile
shone through the dim park lights. "Presidential timber, presidential timber," she said, and after a pause, "Presidential
timber. Such an *American* notion. Rutherford B. Hayes.
James A. Garfield. Chester A. Arthur. Presidential timber."
She looked at me severely. "Of course you wouldn't know
anything about presidential timber. Those presidents and
would-be presidents after the Civil War. No Southerner can
afford to know anything about American history." I hope I
said either nothing or something polite; if something polite
I must have regretted it, for I have forgotten what I may
have said. I had spent four years in the New York Public
Library reading American history and had written two moderately bad books about it to the neglect of James Oliver
Curwood.

Late one bright September morning—it is still 1929—I
strolled down the rue de l'Odéon with no destination in mind,
but stopped a moment in front of Shakespeare & Company,
and then decided to go in. Sylvia stocked American "little
magazines" that could not be found elsewhere in Paris. As
I was greeting her she called out to a man who was about to
leave: "Ernest, come back a minute." I knew at a glance
which Ernest he was. Who would not have known, even then?
—the author of *Three Stories and Ten Poems, The Sun Also
Rises,* and *The Torrents of Spring.* Had one been in the middle
of the Sahara and a wandering Bedouin had suddenly appeared and asked, "Where is Ernest? Where is Robert?" one
would have been in no doubt at all about which Ernest and
which Robert, of all the Ernests and Roberts *in orbe terrarum,*

the Bedouin meant. Sylvia said something like "This is Allen Tate," and the next thing I remember Ernest and I were walking up the rue de l'Odéon towards the Place where we sat on the terrace of the Café Voltaire and, it being midday, ordered two vermouth cassis.

He plunged at once into two of the reviews of his work that I had written for *The Nation* in 1926, in which I implied that he had studied Captain Marryat and Defoe's *Moll Flanders.* "You're wrong about that," he said. "Never heard of Marryat, and never read Defoe." (Some weeks later I mentioned this to John Bishop, who said that around 1923 Ernest kept on his night-table a copy of *Peter Simple* and a dog-eared copy of *Captain Singleton;* so I was only partly wrong.) The talk went amiably on until Ernest suddenly stared at me and said, "You're a friend of Ford, aren't you?" I admitted it, adding that he had lent us his flat last winter. "Well," he said, "you know he's impotent." I was somewhat taken back, but at last said that that must be rather sad for Ford, but not being a women I could feel very little interest in Ford's sexual powers, and was simply grateful for his kindnesses to me. After some desultory talk he asked me whom I knew in Paris; I mentioned a few names and he said that Scott and Zelda would be back soon, and would Caroline and I come to see him and Pauline; they lived five minutes' walk from the Odéon in the rue Ferou. Ernest Hemingway was handsome and even his malice had a certain charm; I couldn't have known then that he was the complete son of a bitch who would later write about certain friends, all of them defenselessly dead, in *A Moveable Feast.* Hemingway himself has now joined them.

From early October until after Christmas, when we sailed for New York, I suppose I saw more of Bishop and Hemingway than of any other persons. I remember a Sunday morning when I heard a timid knock at our third-floor suite of two small rooms. It was Ernest, who without so much as a good morning said I'd better go with him that afternoon to the bicycle races at the Vélodrome d'Hiver. I protested that that sort of thing bored me, that American football was all right, but not bicycles. He kept insisting. And I went, and went with him almost every Sunday for three months; I too became, or almost became, an expert on the *bicylette de course*, especially the *vitesse* and the *demi-fond*. I suppose Ernest liked the *demi-fond* best because the man on the bicycle back of the man on the motorcycle could easily fall off and might get killed. He didn't want people to be killed, only animals; but there was the risk, just as he liked the risk of a matador being killed. I never understood how he felt about bulls; there were, he said, only good bulls and bad bulls.

One morning John Bishop telephoned to say that the Fitzgeralds were back, that he and Margaret were having a dinner party the next week, that the Fitzgeralds and the Hemingways would be there and a few others. We had been dining out occasionally with the Bishops at what I called "compromise restaurants": restaurants below their scale but rather expensive for me. Margaret was of the *haut monde*, or near it, and they lived at a fashionable address near the Etoile during the cold months, leaving their Chateau de Tressancourt at Orgeval, twenty miles from Paris. That handsome villa had been a hunting lodge of Louis XIV; there John and Margaret lived for several years in elegant isolation. At their flat in Paris, later that autumn, Red Warren, who had come over from Oxford, and I spent a long evening with John during which he read us some new poems and the great long story, "Many Thousands Gone." I asked him if his friends Hemingway and Fitzgerald had seen any of his work. He answered no. He read their work as it was written, and his advice was always astute. He was not ambitious; he was modest to a fault; and because he was not competitive, his friends in Paris ignored him. I am certain that the response of Red Warren and myself encouraged him to bring his writing together and publish a few years later the book of stories, *Many Thousands Gone*, and the brilliant volume of poems, *Now With His Love*.

At the Bishops' dinner party there were eight or ten people
—Charlie Sweeney, Ernest and Pauline Hemingway, Pierre de
Lanux and his American wife, and a few others I don't remember after forty years. Somebody said that the Fitzgeralds
were late. I was glad to see Pierre de Lanux, whom I had met
several times before; he had written a short book entitled
Sud, in which for the first time, so far as I knew then, a
Frenchman had understood that the antebellum South might
have had something that men everywhere, until recently,
valued as a civilized society. Then the Fitzgeralds arrived; I
had not met them before. Zelda came forward and we were
introduced: not a beautiful woman but immensely attractive,
with the Southern woman's gift for conversation that made
people feel that she had known them for years. She said that
I must have danced with her at Sewanee. I had to answer no,
that I was some miles away at Vanderbilt. (Zelda had been
a prom-trotter as a debutante.) I remember turning aside and
asking our host where Scott was. John said he was in the
kitchen hiding his bottle of gin, that he would appear in a
moment and drink with us, and then slip out to the kitchen
and reinforce his martini. At last he came in. John introduced
us. After the reciprocal I'm glad to know you, I've heard about
you, he said, "Do you enjoy sleeping with your wife?" I
couldn't believe it; so I said, "What did you say?" He repeated
it. I said, "It's none of your damn business." I turned my
back and walked over to John and, whispering, asked what
in heaven's name Fitzgerald had meant. John said that Scott
asked every man that question, at the first meeting, and that
I should forget it; that any answer, yes or no, or the one I
gave, would condemn me.

I never knew Fitzgerald as well as I knew Hemingway, but
I liked him better, even though he was not as good company;
he was always a little worried about what today we would
call his public image. He once asked me what teenage girls
felt about America. I answered that I didn't know and couldn't
care less. And had they read his *The Beautiful and the*

Damned; and so on. I must have seen him ten or a dozen times in November and December of 1929, the last time I remember being an evening with him and Red Warren, café-crawling in Montmartre. I remember Red saying that he admired *The Great Gatsby.* Scott said, "Say that again and I'll hit you." Red said it again. Scott rose from the table and, putting on Red's overcoat, rushed out and disappeared. The ordeal of getting their overcoats exchanged required several days' effort by me, by John Bishop, and by Red himself. John explained that Scott couldn't bear having his early work praised; that he was then trying to write what became four years later *Tender Is the Night;* and that secretly he feared it would not be better than *Gatsby.* There was a three weeks' *crise d'alcool* after Hemingway bullied him into cabling Max Perkins a lie denying that Morley Callaghan had knocked Hemingway out in a sparring match. Scott kept repeating, blurring the syllables, "What a bastard to cable that lie." One night I escorted him home in a cab three times, miles away near the Etoile; three times, when my cab stopped at my hotel in the Place de l'Odéon, another cab stopped behind it, and Scott stepped out. Only after the fourth trip was I not followed. Scott hero-worshiped Ernest, who I thought took advantage of Scott's insecurities to prove to himself that he was a better writer than Scott. He was not a better writer than Scott; he was not as good a writer. Ernest didn't like other fiction writers but could put up with critics if they admired him (this view I got from John Bishop); and he liked best certain poets, most of all Archie MacLeish, who had been close to Ernest in Paris in the early twenties.

One bright Sunday morning in December, Ernest telephoned and asked me to meet him at eleven at the Deux Magots, that there was something he wanted to tell me. I suspected he was still planning a skiing expedition to the Alps for John and Katie Dos Passos, who were due in Paris in a few days. I had told him that I couldn't go—I was no athlete, I was a physical coward, and so on. He told John Bishop what

I had said, and added: "Allen has *moral* courage." Thus the Hemingway myth was stretched a little for a poet who had not yet written a novel, and for a critic who, in spite of mentioning Marryat and Defoe, admired him.

I arrived at the Deux Magots a few minutes late and found him huddled over a brazier on the terrace facing St. Germain des Prés. He had ordered a coffee for me. He said, "Look at this," and handed me the *Paris Herald*, pointing to a picture on the front page. It was President Hoover in a boat, fishing, and wearing a high starched collar and tie. "This fellow," Ernest said, "will never do anything for the likes of you and me." I suppose I laughed. Then he was silent; I began to wonder what he wanted to tell me. He said, "Don't make too much love while you're young; save up some for middle age." Was this what he wanted to discuss? He was silent again. He obviously didn't want to tell me what he had decided to tell me. Finally I said something like, "What's on your mind?", to which he replied, "Gertrude has taken me back into favor." I must have thought, "Well, what of it?" Then Ernest came out with it. "I'm taking Pauline to rue de Fleurus this evening, and I want other people to be there. You and Caroline, along with the Fitzgeralds and the Bishops; they've all agreed to come." And they all did come along, except, I believe, Margaret Bishop.

We arrived all together around nine and were admitted by Miss Toklas, who forthwith asked the ladies to follow her to the rear of the Grand Salon. This was the usual procedure *chez* Stein. The ladies were, of course, second-class citizens, and segregated around a table to be entertained by Miss Toklas, while Miss Stein engaged the men—or perhaps I may say gentlemen—in the corner of the salon to the right of the entrance. I was astonished to see Ford there; he was facing his hostess from a low chair, one of a half-circle of chairs around Miss Stein, who was about to preside from a large American overstuffed chair. What Ford was doing there I couldn't imagine, and I never found out. Surely Hemingway

had not asked him to come. We—the gentlemen—were ordered to sit down. I noticed that Ernest sat as far back as
possible; but I sat directly facing our hostess. When I have
not seen a picture of Miss Stein for some time, I find myself
thinking how handsome she was, a little like Richard Burton
in the role of Becket. About twenty Picassos looked down
from three walls of the salon. One never looked up at them
because one's attention was all for their collector.

The program for that warm December evening was a lecture, or short course in American literature, beginning with
Washington Irving, whose works Miss Stein did not distinguish very clearly from those of James Fenimore Cooper.
However that may have been, Irving was really European,
she said, being concerned with local color and experience,
whereas the true genius of America was for abstraction.
Emerson was a forerunner, but after Emerson there was only
the sad case of Henry James, whose novels had abstract de-
sign but were ruined by his getting bogged down in the
American experience of Europe. She suddenly looked at Ford.
"Ford," she said, "simply won't do." And nobody laughed.
Ford stared from his fish-like eyes, his mouth open not for
speech but for air. There was a silence. I had supposed silence
in company was rude, so I foolishly said, "How interesting,
Miss Stein." She looked sternly at me. "Nonsense, my dear
Tate, nonsense." She evidently had not heard what I had
said, but thought I was contradicting her. For a moment I
was tempted to believe that she was reading my mind, for I
definitely thought that what she had said about abstraction,
Henry James, and Ford was nonsense; and that she was agree-
ing with me. But no—the lecture was resumed, the climax of
which, the entelechy towards which all American literature
was striving, I need not describe, for the reader has already
perceived it. At the end of the lecture Miss Stein rose; we all
got up; and amid the babble of goodnights the ladies came
forward from their compound, having had tea and good American chocolate cake. We all walked down the rue de Fleurus

to the rue Guynemer and the Luxembourg, under the bright December moon. Scott Fitzgerald walked on ahead, alone, and I heard him say, "I have seen Shelley plain." My continuing education ground to a halt. What could one make of that— from the best American novelist of his generation? And it suddenly came to me that Hemingway and Miss Stein, on the occasion of his restoration to favor, had not exchanged one word. Oh, yes, Miss Toklas' American cake. I didn't have any that evening; I never got any at the numerous Thursdays; I never got anything, not even much education.

These trivia have survived a world that is dead for the entertainment of a world that is dying. *Sunt lacrimae rerum et mentem mortalia tangunt.*

Memories of Sylvia Beach

1962

I DON'T REMEMBER "meeting" Sylvia Beach. In the autumn of 1928, shortly after I had arrived in Paris, I began to drop in at Shakespeare and Company to look at the American and British journals, and occasionally to buy a book. By the time I left Paris in January 1930 Sylvia and I had become good friends. I saw a good deal of her again in 1932 when I went back to Paris. It was good to see Adrienne Monnier. Sylvia was kind to me from the beginning. I never knew why, except that true kindness needs no reason. When my wife and I left Paris again early in 1933, Sylvia and Adrienne gave us a delightful dinner party at Adrienne's apartment. All I remember was the warmth and the lively talk, and one remark of Adrienne's: "Monsieur Tate is so conservative that he's almost radical." It was a warning that I hope I have profited by these thirty years.

I didn't see Sylvia again (I never saw Adrienne Monnier again) until 1952, but it was only a glimpse; I was a "delegate" to a large international conference at which everybody was talking all the time and saying virtually nothing. At an official reception we did talk a few minutes. She told me she had a manuscript of mine that Archie MacLeish had left with her in 1927. I asked her to destroy it. She gently refused; and then I told her to keep it. (I couldn't have borne the shock of seeing some of those early poems, no other copies of which existed.) I didn't see her again until 1956.

That was at the American Embassy in Paris, on a cold December morning, at a lecture I was giving the embassy staff. There she was, in the front row, and I was greatly moved by her kindness in coming to listen to me. I was in Paris some days longer, and saw her almost every day, either at her flat or with the Jackson Mathews. She was by then well along in years, but I saw no loss in vitality of person or of mind. And she never forgot anything or any person to whom she had given her friendship. After 1956 I saw her only three times.

I was in Paris in the spring of 1959 when her famous collection of books and manuscripts of the twenties was being shown by the USIS in the rue du Dragon. One of my most prized mementoes is a picture of Sylvia and myself taken in front of the case in which some of my books were exhibited. At that time I was fifty-nine years old, and the melancholy conceit that I was the youngest person included in the show depressed me for several days. Where did that put all the others? Our time was running out, but I could not know that Sylvia's, although I knew her age, would come so soon. I saw her twice again, but briefly, in Paris in 1961 and later that year with the Jackson Mathews in New York after she had got her honorary degree at Buffalo. I don't like to remember those last meetings. I might have thanked her, but I never got around to thanking her for the kindnesses she had shown an unknown young man who came to Shakespeare and Company in the rue de l'Odéon in 1928.

John Peale Bishop

1948

ON THE EVENING of September 23, 1925, I was dining with Hart Crane in a speakeasy on Washington Place in New York. Towards the end of dinner I saw Kenneth Burke and another man at the far end of the restaurant, and, when Crane left for another engagement, I went over to speak to Burke. He introduced me to John Peale Bishop. I remember the time and circumstances because Burke made a joke about my having become a father on that day. I was a little excited and concerned with myself; I remember very little of Bishop from the hour I sat at their table. I could not suspect then that the meeting was the beginning of a long and affectionate friendship. We did not meet again until 1928, in Paris.

John Peale Bishop was born in Charles Town, West Virginia, in the Shenandoah Valley, on May 21, 1892, the son of Jonathan Peale Bishop and Margaret Miller Cochran. On his mother's side he came of stock that had settled in Virginia in the late seventeenth and early eighteenth centuries. This Tidewater ancestry, moving westward at about the close of the French and Indian War to what was then the frontier in the Valley of Virginia, mingled with the new German and

Scotch-Irish strains that had begun to pour into the valley from Pennsylvania and the Carolinas just before the Revolution. His mother carried with her two centuries of the history of Virginia. At fourteen John copied from Waddell's *Annals of Augusta County* the names of his family connections that had fought in the Indian wars and the Revolution: Moffett, Warwick, Breckinridge, McDowell, McClanahan. With these Scotch and English families the Germans were mingled; the Millers, or Müllers, had founded in the late 1750s the town of Müllerstadt, later Woodstock, in Shenandoah County, in the lower, northern end of the valley. But Bishop's father was of Connecticut descent, and had been brought as a child to Charles Town, where, I suppose, he always remained an outsider, being a Yankee. Bishop's beautiful poem, "Beyond Connecticut, Beyond the Sea," recovers an ancestral past from which his Southern upbringing had cut him off. Years ago he told me that as a boy his father had been "stoned in the streets." The phrase appears in his poem. In Bishop there was a deep conflict of loyalties felt by many people in the border South from 1865 to 1914, and I think it is one key to the understanding of his work.

He was nine when his father died, and his mother soon remarried. In his last ten years it seemed to me, when we talked about such matters, as we more and more did, that he more and more took imaginatively the part of his father, of the outsider, of the *déraciné*. It was a role that merged very early in his life with that of the modern romantic poet. That he was fully conscious of the historical beginnings of this split in loyalty (it became later the condition of his special sensibility, liberating his powers of observation) is quite plain in the fine story, "Many Thousands Gone," in which the Yankee officer occupying the Virginia town of Mordington (Charles Town) is himself a native of Mordington who has taken the side of the "enemy." He is described as having sandy hair, a small moustache, and a fox-like face. I have always seen in this portrait a caricature of Bishop himself.

His boyhood seems to have been that of most boys in a small Southern town. At an early age he became interested in birds and before he was ten he had written a birdbook, the manuscript of which his sister has preserved. It became a life-long interest. In his last years he always took his field-glasses when he went walking, and the seabirds of Cape Cod were a constant delight to him. He discovered an aquatic bird long supposed by ornithologists to be extinct. His sister, Mrs. Allen Myers, tells me that John "declaimed poetry at all hours" when he was a schoolboy, and knew hundreds of lines; in high school he won an oratorical contest. I can see in this the origin of his pleasure in speaking well, and in the inter-minable "elevated" talk of the Southern family at the turn of the century perhaps the origin of the noble diction of his verse: like the other Southern poets of his generation he was something of a rhetorician who never felt the influences here or abroad which later made possible the more colloquial lan-guage of the British poets Auden and MacNeice. His sister recalls the good times he had when he was young—the round of parties and dances in Charles Town and the towns nearby: in later years he told her that he didn't know whether all the girls he knew in his boyhood were pretty, but he thought they were.

His education after the elementary stage was all in the North. He attended the Mercersburg Academy in Pennsyl-vania, and was graduated from Princeton in 1917 when he was twenty-five. He was thus older than his friends Wilson and Fitzgerald, and his undergraduate writings, though derivative, have a precision and finish that undergraduates seldom achieve. In World War I he was a first lieutenant of infantry in the 84th Division, and remained in Europe until 1919 in command of a detachment guarding German prisoners. When he came back he went on *Vanity Fair*, later succeeding Ed-mund Wilson as managing editor. Between 1919 and 1922 he wrote the verse and prose pieces which became his part in *The Undertaker's Garland* (1922). On June 17, 1922, he was married to Margaret Grosvenor Hutchins, of a Columbus, Ohio family, and went to live abroad, in Paris and Sorrento; in this period he first knew Ezra Pound, E. E. Cummings, and Archibald MacLeish.

It was his first residence abroad, and, more than his earlier war experience, it sharpened his sense of the relation of America to Europe, and even of the relation of the South to the North. Here began the consciousness of the past in the present out of which grew his most important work. From 1924 to 1925 he was again in New York, on the staff of Paramount Pictures. In 1926 he returned to France, settling in an old house about twenty kilometers to the northeast of Paris—the Chateau du Petit Tressancourt in the village of Orgèval. There the Bishops lived some seven years, and my own frequent visits to Tressancourt between 1928 and 1930, and again in 1932, made it obvious to me that he had not been happy in that charming isolation. More dependent upon a sympathetic literary society than most writers, he seemed in that period remote and without concentration, except at intervals when he produced, in a burst of energy, a group of poems or an occasional story. It was my impression that he felt he ought to produce a popular work: I think he worked for a while at a musical comedy. A wit of the Bishops' circle said to me one day that "John is like a man lying in a warm bath who faintly hears the telephone ringing downstairs."

This was his condition when I arrived in Paris in 1928. On a December evening of that year he read to Robert Penn Warren and me a story, the first draft of "Many Thousands Gone," and I asked him, "Has anybody seen it?" "No," he said. I knew that his friends were constantly bringing him their work, but apparently nobody read his. He had a special modesty and detachment and a generosity which people took for granted in that time of highly developed literary "personalities" and competitive literary careers. In the twenties, in Paris and New York, few people read anything, even the books which presumably had made the reputations of the writers most talked about. I am not the right person to go into this mystery of literary fashion; yet I ought to say that John Bishop was distinctly not the fashion. He had little gift for dramatizing himself as a literary personality, and I always suspected that his dandyism, a sort of social mask behind which he concealed himself, was his way of withdrawing from the literary scene, perhaps an expression of contempt for the literary *arriviste*. (This mask, of course, had its own defects; I think it limited his range as a writer.) His closest friends at that time, Hemingway, Fitzgerald, and MacLeish, were distinctly not *arrivistes*. Yet I felt that nobody in Paris quite took him seriously as a writer. The writings of all these men, and of others, including myself, would have been the poorer without his disinterested advice: he had a quick intuitive sense of the problems involved in his friends' work.

In 1933 the Bishops returned to America to live, first in New Orleans for a year, then in Connecticut; and in 1938 they built a house at South Chatham, Massachusetts, on Cape Cod, where they lived until John's death in 1944. Here he lived again in the isolation that he had known at Orgèval. Between 1936, when *Minute Particulars* appeared, and 1940, when Scott Fitzgerald died, he produced very little poetry, yet he wrote in those years some of his best critical essays, "The Discipline of Poetry," "The Sorrows of Thomas Wolfe," and "Poetry and Painting." The death of Fitzgerald was the occasion of the elegy, "The Hours," and indirectly of numerous short poems which are among his best, as well as the fine long poem, "A Subject of Sea Change." Early in 1941 he came to New York as Publications Director of the Office of the Coordinator of Inter-American Affairs, where he planned and put through some of the best South American anthologies; here he invited me to collaborate with him in a United States anthology to be translated into Spanish for the South American republics, and I saw him constantly. He seemed in the year and a half he thus spent in New York to regain something of his old enthusiasm for literature (I had felt a withdrawal in the two or three years before 1941), but his health was not good and the high blood pressure that he had had for many years was getting worse. He went back to South Chatham in June 1942.

In the next year and a half I did not see him, being in the South; but when I saw him again, in November 1943, he had aged greatly. It is not too much to say that the war hastened his death. Not being a man of action he had few of the public outlets which some of his friends seized to get themselves through the inner crisis which the war created in us all. In October 1943, I had suggested to Archie MacLeish, who was then Librarian of Congress, that John would be the right man to fill the new post of Resident Fellow in Comparative Literature in the Library; and MacLeish acted at once. But when John arrived in Washington early in November he was obviously ill. At the end of two weeks he had a heart attack and had to go home. I put him on the train, and, had I known how ill he was, I would have gone with him. After a few weeks he seemed to get better, and late that winter was able to walk a little; but in March he grew weaker and by the middle of March his wife knew that the end was not far away. A few days before he died Margaret telephoned me and I asked her whether it might please John to have me sit with him: she told me that he could no longer recognize me or anybody else. On April 4, 1944, he died.

About a week before his death, becoming conscious for a while, he told Margaret that he had been blessed with "wonderful friends" and that his life had not been wasted. We who survive him into a world that he could not have liked are, I think, even better judges of that than he. The names of the friends he mentioned in the last conscious hour it pleases me to put down as he spoke them to his wife: "Bunny, Allen, and Archie." Not least among John's gifts was the gift of distinguished friendship. In that same talk he dictated to Margaret his epitaph:

Long did I live
Consistent, lonely, proud.
Not death, but fear of death,
Restores us to the crowd.

Homage to St.-John Perse

1950

I FIRST SAW St.-John Perse in the autumn of 1943, when I called upon him in the Library of Congress in Washington. He was at his desk in a bare cubicle, compiling bibliographies of recent French literature for the use of the library staff in enlarging the collections of French books. We were both "employees" of the library; we had come there, he into exile, I from one exile to another, after the manner of Americans, who are never more exiled than when they are "at home." We had come at the invitation of our friend Archibald MacLeish, then the Librarian of Congress, who has done more than any other American to convey to our public the quality of St.-John Perse's art and the image of the man. I shall not forget that first meeting. I was a stranger whose name he had never heard, and this was a test of his courtesy, which was perfect. We talked a few minutes, and made an engagement for lunch a few days hence. From that luncheon conversation on he became to me Alexis, and we have been friends ever since.

His courage, his patience, his dignity, amid what must have been the profound and even tragic crisis which he was then suffering and which he perhaps suffers still, though with what victories the astonishing series of poems from "Exil" to "Vents" reveals to us: these qualities of courage, patience, and dignity are but the outward sign of a self-mastery which directs, controls, and illuminates the poems. It is difficult, I think, to speak more definitely of these matters, which seem to me nevertheless to be of the first importance. They must remain mysterious. Now that the mystery of "St.-John Perse" has been dissolved in the revelation of Alexis St. Leger Leger, we have only exchanged a lesser for a greater mystery: the more we know about the man, the deeper the mystery of his unique art.

For the American reader, perhaps also for the English, certain dissociations must be made before one can even begin to read the poems. When T. S. Eliot's paraphrase of "Anabase" first appeared (1930) one might carelessly try to place the originality and hitherto unknown power of the work in a wholly irrelevant setting, derived from sources in English. One thought of the exoticism of the late James Elroy Flecker (an accomplished minor English poet) and of the long, unmetrical line, swelling frequently to lines grouped as short paragraphs, of Walt Whitman. The association with Whitman was the more misleading in that Whitman *seems* to share with Perse the vast reach of allusion and the sudden descent of the eye to the particular object; one must also refer to the trap set for the American reader by the "exoticism" of a work like Whitman's "Passage to India." I do not know whether Perse has read Whitman, but I can well believe that his poetry, if Whitman had never written, would be exactly what it is today. No actual comparison of Perse with Whitman is possible; yet the two influences (Whitman by way of Carl Sandburg) unite in Perse's friend Archibald MacLeish. Because such a fusion has been possible, it is important, I believe, to sharpen one's sense of the differences. I quote from *Song of Myself:*

Come now I will not be tantalized, you conceive too
  much of articulation,

Do you not know O speech how the buds beneath
  you are folded?

Waiting in gloom, protected by frost,

The dirt receding before my prophetical screams,

I underlying causes to balance them at last,

My knowledge my live parts, it keeps tally with the
  meaning of all things,

Happiness (which whoever hears me let him or her
  set out in search of this day).

The passage is a reproach addressed to Language as if the
tongue were a coy and intractable woman. Like many single
passages from Whitman it seems to be a mixture of commonplace and obscurity unless one keeps in mind the mounting impact of the whole poem: an impact due less to depth
of perspective opened up by the images than to the hypnotic
power of the personal rhythm. (This similarity between
Whitman and Ezra Pound in the *Cantos* has never been
explored.) Something like the reverse of this poetic method
seems to account for the peculiar power of St.-John Perse.

A glance at three of the later poems will reveal such profound differences from Whitman that superficial resemblances
become inconsiderable. The rhythms of "Pluies," "Neiges,"
and "Vents" are not like anything that we know in English
as "free verse." In French (an unaccented language) we hear,
in non-metrical poetry, the cadence and the rhythms which
are the result of phrase-sequence and phrase-length; so that
there is never—at least in Perse—the effect of a merely de-
teriorated metrical line, such as we sometimes hear in Whitman.

Qu'elles descendent, tertres sacrés, au bas du ciel
couleur d'anthrax et de sanie, avec les fleuves sous
leurs bulles tirant leur charge d'alluents, tirant leur
chaine de membranes et d'anses et de grandes pla-
centaires—toute la treille de leurs sources et le grand
arbre capillaire jusqu'en ses prolongements de
veines, de veinules. ...

This passage, taken almost at random from "Vents," is typical
of Perse's freedom from the semi-metrical line. The very
grammar, which reflects through the repetition of *tirant* a
rhetorical extension into a precise, unpredictable aspect of
the image, becomes itself a principle of organization. In spite
of the synesthetic imagery of much of Perse's poetry, and the
superficial likeness not only to Whitman but to Rimbaud, we
have here from a modern Frenchman a series of powerful
poems the units of which resemble, in structure, the historic
verse-paragraph which was the most original rhetorical invention of John Milton.

These parallels in English, even if they be just, will possibly
bore the French reader; but it would be a mistake for a critic
in English (or, at any rate, for the present writer) to try to
look at Perse from inside his own traditions. We must use both
French and Anglo-American poetry, and allow for mistakes
of reference. (I doubt that we do so badly with French literature, on the whole, as the French do with us. We are at least
able to distinguish Bernanos from Mauriac, whereas the
French seem not to know the difference between Faulkner
and Steinbeck: both are American barbarians.) It is beyond
my capacity, as it would be an impertinence on this occasion,
to discuss Perse's relation to Valéry and Claudel, the only
French poets of his time who to the eye of an American
reader seem to be his peers. Perse once made a remark to me
about Valéry in connection with a long formalistic poem of
my own. It was to the effect that the greater concreteness
and intractability of English imposed certain formal neces-

sities upon our poetry. The less physical French language
tended too easily to attract formal effects, and that possibly
Valéry had exhausted, for our age, the French formal limits.
A return of the French language to the sensibility, and of
poetic rhythms to inchoate verse, had become a necessity.

How far any poet may be trusted to deliver objective judgments on the verse of other poets (I suspect my own) will
remain an unsettled problem. I have mentioned Perse's comment on Valéry only to observe that his sensitivity to language, both French and English, is wonderfully acute, and
that his knowledge of English poetry is so broad and exact
that quite possibly a large general English influence must be
acknowledged in a poet completely French. Is it not thoroughly French to assimilate a wide range of cultures, ground
them in the French sensibility, and forget that they ever came
from over the frontier? There are, for example, two Poes: one
is named Poe and the other Poë. The Frenchman Poë would
not recognize his American counterpart should they pass each
other in the street.

It seems to me inevitable that "Vents" will take its place
with "Le Cimitière Marin" as a landmark in modern poetry
in any language. How long a poem will "last" nobody had
better try to decide. Yet "Vents," with the two other poems,
"Pluies" and "Neiges," which likewise develop with great
power meteorological imagery, establishes for our generation
a location of the spirit that once known must be returned to
again. Here we have man under the elements, and the elements in man, who yields to them. But the broadest of these
powerful symbols which reach us through the sensibility
rather than the intellect, is the wind: at one level it is the
Dantesque wind of the Second Circle; it expands into the
driven spirit of man in his present distress. It would be a
mistake if we stopped, at that point, our exploration of the
symbol: we should be stopping at its romantic implications.
The beautiful symmetry of the form, the precision of image,
and the presence of a cold and passionate intelligence com-

bine in a quality of insight which is not of the provincial rationalism of our time. It reaffirms the greater tradition of the tragic consciousness.

William Faulkner
1897-1962

1962

I AM WRITING this memoir, or perhaps it had better be called an obituary, in Italy, where it is so difficult to find William Faulkner's books that I have not even tried. But at one time or another I have read them all except *Knight's Gambit* and *The Reivers*, and it is probably better, on this occasion, to rely upon one's memory than to try to read again and "revaluate" the greater books. I am not sure of what I am about to write, but I am thinking of it as recollection and appreciation, not criticism; yet without what amounts to a profound admiration of his works (this is a kind of criticism) I should not have accepted the editor's invitation to write about William Faulkner at all. For in the thirty-one years of our acquaintance I saw him not more than five or six times, and but for one meeting in Rome about ten years ago he seemed to me arrogant and ill-mannered in a way that I felt qualified to distinguish as peculiarly "Southern": in company he usually failed to reply when spoken to, or when he spoke there was something grandiose in the profusion with which he sprinkled his remarks with "Sirs" and "Ma'ms." Years ago, when I was editing *The Sewanee Review*, I had some correspondence with him; his letters were signed "Faulk-

---

This obituary appeared in *The New Statesman*.

ner." I wrote him that English nobility followed this practice and I never heard from him again.

I suppose the main source of my annoyance with him was his affectation of not being a writer, but a farmer; this would have been pretentious even had he been a farmer. But being a "farmer," he did not "associate" with writers—with the consequence that he was usually surrounded by third-rate writers or just plain sycophants. Excepting Malcolm Cowley he was not a friend of anybody who could conceivably have been his peer.

One may leave the man to posterity, but the work must be reread now, and talked about, lest Faulkner, like other writers of immense fame in their lifetimes, go into a slump. However great a writer may be, the public gets increasingly tired of him; his death seems to remove the obligation to read him. But if I had read *The Reivers*, I should be willing to say something about the work as a whole, and an essay would make some of the points that I can only suggest in this "obituary" of a man I did not like, but of a writer who since the early thirties I have thought was the greatest American novelist after Henry James: a novelist of an originality and power not equalled by his contemporaries, Hemingway and Fitzgerald.

Leaving aside the two books that I have not read, I should say that he wrote at least five great novels (what other American novelist wrote so many, except James?): they are *The Sound and the Fury, As I Lay Dying, Sanctuary, Light in August*, and *The Hamlet*. I know people of good judgment who would add to this list *The Wild Palms* and *Absalom, Absalom!*, books that contain some great writing but that in the end are not novels. Of the four first titles on my list, none appeared after 1932; the fifth, in 1940. *Absalom, Absalom!* and *The Wild Palms* came out in 1936 and 1939. All Faulkner's seven great books were written in a span of about eleven or twelve years. The fine long story "The Bear" was written towards the end of this period. The later books round out the picture of Yoknapatawpha County (Lafayette County, Mississippi), but nobody would know them had the earlier books not been written. William Faulkner wrote only one bad novel, *A Fable*, his version of the Grand Inquisitor, contrived in theological ignorance and placed in a setting that he had not observed.

Observation of scene is the phrase that will take us closer than any other to the mystery of Faulkner's genius. The three plots of *Light in August* are all in synopsis incredible, but we believe them at last, or accept them as probable, because the characters are in the first place credible. The famous violence of William Faulkner is a violence of character, not of action; there are, of course, violent "scenes"; yet these scenes, like the murder of Joe Christmas in *Light in August*, or the Bundren family crossing the swollen river with Addie's coffin, all add up to a powerful "direct impression of life" which Henry James said some eighty years ago would be the province of the novel. I am not indulging myself in paradox when I say that nothing "happens" in *The Sound and the Fury*, just as nothing happens in *Madame Bovary*: in both novels there are famous suicides. Yet Quentin Compson's death, though it comes before the end of the book, is the last brushstroke in the portrait of the Compson family; and likewise the suicide of Emma Bovary rounds out a picture, not an action.

The European reader finds something uniquely American in Faulkner, and obviously no European could have written his books; the few European commentators that I have read seem to me to glorify William Faulkner in a provincial American (or Southern) vacuum. I believe that as his personality fades from view he will be recognized as one of the last great craftsmen of the art of fiction which Ford Madox Ford called the impressionist novel. From Stendhal through Flaubert and Joyce there is a direct line to Faulkner, and it is not a mere question of influence. Faulkner's great subject, as it was Flaubert's and Proust's, is passive suffering, the victim being destroyed either by society or by dark forces within himself. Faulkner is one of the great exemplars of the international school of fiction which for more than a century has reversed the Aristotelian doctrine that tragedy is an action, not a quality.

William Faulkner's time and place made it possible for him to extend this European tradition beyond any boundaries that were visible to novelists of New England, the Middle West, or the Far West. The Greco-Trojan myth (Northerners as the upstart Greeks, Southerners as the older, more civilized Trojans) presented Faulkner, before he had written a line, with a large semihistorical background against which even his ignorant characters, like Lena Grove or Dewey Dell Bundren, as well as the more civilized Compsons and Sartorises, could be projected in more than human dimensions. I had occasion some years ago to say in the *New Statesman* that had William Faulkner invented his myth, it could not have been as good as it turned out to be (Sophocles was doubtless in a similarly advantageous position with respect to the Oedipean cycle). Faulkner brought to bear upon the myth greater imaginative powers than any of his contemporaries possessed; but he was not unique; for it is only further evidence of his greatness that he wrote in an age when there were other Southern novelists almost as good: Robert Penn Warren, Caroline Gordon, Andrew Lytle, Stark Young, Eudora Welty, Katherine Anne Porter—and Faulkner would have included Thomas Wolfe, though I did not credit his honesty when he placed Wolfe at the top of his contemporaries. (He never mentioned the others.)

Two secondary themes in Faulkner have obscured the critics' awareness of the great theme. These are: the white man's legacy of guilt for slavery and the rape of the land. These themes are almost obsessive, but they are not the main theme. William Faulkner was not a "segregationist." (Whether he was an "integrationist" is a different question.) But how could he not have been a segregationist when he said that he would shoot Negroes in the streets if the Federal Government interfered in Mississippi? Unless the European —or for that matter the Northern—reader understands that for Faulkner, and for the thousands of other Southerners of his generation, the separatism and possible autonomy of the South came before all other "problems," he will misread Faulkner because he will not have discerned the great theme. I will repeat it in different language: the destruction of the Old South released native forces of disorder and corruption which were accelerated by the brutal exploitation of the Carpetbaggers and an army of occupation; thus the old order of dignity and principle was replaced by upstarts and cynical materialists. Federal interference in the South had brought this about; and when Faulkner said he would shoot Negroes if that were necessary to keep Federal interference at bay, his response came directly out of the Greco-Trojan myth; and yet it was the response of a man who had depicted Negroes with greater understanding and compassion than any other Southern writer of his time.

William Faulkner is, I think, with Hawthorne and James in the United States, and one of the great company in Europe that I have mentioned. He was a great writer. We shall not see his like again in our time.

Homage to T. S. Eliot

1966

A FEW DAYS AFTER January 4th of last year I knew that I needed to do something about the loss I was becoming more and more aware of in the death of T. S. Eliot. On the afternoon of the 4th a reporter at *The New York Times* had telephoned me in Minneapolis and asked me for an "estimate of Mr. Eliot's place in modern literature"—and had I known him and could I think of any interesting anecdotes? This crass incident delayed the shock of realization; and it was several days later that I understood that T. S. Eliot was dead. One dies every day one's own death, but one cannot imagine the death of the man who was *il maestro di color che sanno*—or, since he was an artist and not, after his young manhood, a philosopher: *il maestro di color che scrivonno*. To see his *maestro*, Dante had to "lift his eyelids a little higher," and that was what I knew, after January 4th, I had been doing in the thirty-six years of an acquaintance that almost imperceptibly became friendship. *I looked up to him*, and in doing so I could not feel myself in any sense diminished. What he thought of "us"—by us, I mean his old but slightly younger literary friends—we

87

never quite knew because he never quite said. The un-Eliot or anti-Eliot people thought that his literary reticence was "cagey" and ungenerous. It was the highest form of civility. If he didn't know whether we were good writers it was because he didn't know, in spite of his immense fame, whether he himself would last. Somewhere, in print, he put himself with Yeats. But would Yeats last? I am sure he didn't know. He was simply aware—and he would have been obtuse had he not been aware—that he and Yeats dominated poetry in English in this century; but that, to a deeply empirical mind, meant little in the long run of posterity.

What, then, could I do? On the death of a friend one may meditate the Thankless Muse, even if the friend was not a poet. The meditation becomes more difficult, and one almost gives it up, if the friend is not only a poet but perhaps a great poet. The poet-as-Greatness is not, as our friend might have said in his Harvard dissertation on F. H. Bradley, an object of knowledge: it is only a point of view. Private meditation at best must land one in the midst of The Last Things, beyond the common reality; but poetry begins with the common reality, and ends with it, as our friend's friend, Charles Williams, said of Dante. It could be equally said of Tom Eliot; and that is why it is not inappropriate, on this occasion, to see him first as a man, and to speak plainly of him as Tom; for he was the uncommon man committed to the common reality of the human condition. Only men so committed, and so deeply committed that there is no one moment in their lives when they are aware of an act of commitment, express the perfect simplicity of manners that was Tom Eliot's. There were times when he was silent: I remember a luncheon at a London club, at which Bonamy Dobrée and Herbert Read were also present, when he was *withdrawn*; but he was not withdrawn from us; he was withdrawn into himself. This, too, I take to be a form of civility. Among friends one has the privilege of saying nothing; the civility consists in the assumption that one's silence will be civilly understood. I can imagine a small gathering of friends who say nothing all evening: they recoil from saying anything that the others don't want to hear; and their silence would be the subtlest courtesy.

What—I repeat the question—what, then, could I do? What could I do about the loss I felt in the death not of Tom Eliot but of T. S. Eliot? I almost distinguish the two persons because my friendship with Tom Eliot was a private matter to which the public might have indirect access only if I were capable of writing a formal pastoral elegy like "Lycidas"; but then Tom Eliot would become T. S. Eliot the public figure, a figure considerably larger than his elegist. Is it not customary for the greater man to appropriate the elegiac mode to celebrate the hitherto unknown talents of the lesser? Had Milton's friend King been a great poet Milton could not have *somewhat* loudly swept the strings: he might have been tempted to indulge in hyperbole instead of what he did, which was to forget King, as posterity was to forget him, and give us Milton. Whatever I might do about Tom Eliot or T. S. Eliot, I could not forget him and exhibit the dubious poetic virtuosity of Tate.

What I could do is what I have done, for what one does reveals the limit of what one can do. I have brought together, at the invitation of the editor of *The Sewanee Review*, some twenty essays in reminiscence and appreciation. But there is no invasion of the severe privacy which Tom Eliot the man and T. S. Eliot the poet maintained throughout his seventy-six years. His poems came out of the fiery crucible of his interior life; yet all of the interior life that we know is in the poems; and that is as it should be: for his theory of the impersonality of poetry met no contradiction in the intensely personal origins of the poems. When I asked his old friends to write essays I hoped that they would bear witness to the part that his character and mind had played in their lives and works.

My own fragmentary writings, I think, bear this sort of

witness; yet I surmise that we became friends because I
never tried to imitate him or become a disciple. He abhorred
disciples and his imitators bored him. My other master in
literature, John Crowe Ransom, who is within a few months
of Eliot's age, different as the two men are, has always
treated his younger friends as if we were his equals; we had
to accept equality even though we knew we did not deserve
it. We must be friends or nothing. The high civility of Eliot
and Ransom has almost disappeared from the republic of
letters. Its disappearance means the reduction of the republic
to a raw democracy of competition and aggression, or of
"vanity and impudence." (I borrow the phrase from I. A.
Richards' moving tribute to his old friend.)

This meditation has been difficult to write. I have not been
consistent in my attempt to distinguish Tom Eliot from T. S.
Eliot; perhaps I should not have tried. As I look back upon
the thirty-six years of our friendship I see that Tom gradually
emerged from T. S., forming a double image of a unified mind
and sensibility. I first met him in London in 1928, at one of
the *Criterion* luncheons, to which Herbert Read had invited
me and to which Frank Morley took me. There had been
some formal correspondence as early as 1923 concerning some
of my early poems which he had declined to publish in *The
Criterion*. Years later, in 1956, when he was my guest in
Minneapolis, I showed him his first letter to me in which he
said that I ought to try to "simplify" myself—advice I was
never able to take, try as I would. When he had finished
reading the letter, with that sober attention that he always
gave to the most trivial request of a friend, looking over his
spectacles, he said: "It seems awfully pompous and conde-
scending"; and then he laughed. His laugh was never hearty;
it was something between a chuckle and a giggle; and now
he was laughing both at himself and at me—at me for what
he evidently considered the absurdity of keeping a letter of
his all those years.

In the autumn of 1958 I was at tea with him and his wife

Valerie at their flat in Kensington Court Gardens. I arrived a little late and mumbling an apology said that I had had a late lunch with The Honorable. . . . He was a member of a millionaire American family that had migrated to England in the 1870s or 80s and had been ennobled. Tom (not T. S.) smiled and glanced at his wife. He said: *"We* had not heard of *them* before the War Between the States." I suppose I must explain this sectional joke. Tom Eliot, as everybody knows, was of New England origin, and would not have called that war the War Between the States had I not been present. He was telling his wife and me that he thought those people "newcomers," but he was slyly attributing the prejudice to me as a Southerner who might be supposed to take an unfavorable view of New York millionaires. I cannot think of a better example of the complex simplicity of his humor; and British as be became in many ways, his humor was unmistakably American.

II
OPINIONS

To Cleanth Brooks

Robert Frost as
Metaphysical Poet

1974

ROBERT FROST, "like other poets who have written
with narrow views, and paid court to temporary preju-
dices, has been at one time too much praised, and too
much neglected at another." I have substituted Robert Frost
for Abraham Cowley in this quotation from Johnson's *Life
of Cowley*: the sentence introduces the critical discussion of
Cowley's poems and of certain other poets whom Johnson
mistakenly called "metaphysical," as mistakenly as I have
called Frost a metaphysical poet. Everybody knows that
Johnson meant by "metaphysical" something like abstruse,
complex, difficult. But so is Robert Frost difficult in his own
way. What looks like simplicity will turn out to be—or so
my reading of him tells me—mere simplicity at the surface,
below which lies a *selva obscura* that I shall be able to point
to without quite getting inside it. And I must say here at
the outset that I am not alluding to Mr. Lionel Trilling's
famous eighty-fifth birthday speech, even though I agree with
it: it was the first critical effort to break through the Chinese
Wall of Frostian adulation.

Although I am aware that I am beginning with the negative

Given as a lecture at the Library of Congress on the centenary of
Frost's birth, March 26, 1974.

side of my observations on Robert Frost, I must go a little further and confess that Frost was not, when I was a young man, my kind of poet; nor is he now that I am an old man; and yet I am convinced that he wrote some of the finest poems of our time, or of any time. The Earl of Rochester wrote some of the best short poems in the language; but he is not my kind of poet. I am not linking Rochester and Frost; I am merely saying that one may admire what is not entirely sympathetic: and by not sympathetic I could mean that perhaps the poet wouldn't unreservedly like me.

Now, eleven years after his death, he is in partial eclipse. And nine years after his death, T. S. Eliot is equally in the penumbra of a declining reputation. One expects this immediately after the death of a famous writer. One wonders whether an occasion, such as this centenary celebration, will restore some of the popularity that Robert Frost enjoyed for almost fifty years.

Is the living voice, back of the printed line, necessary? During his lifetime his readers could see, synesthetically, back of the poems they were reading, the handsome, massive face of the master and the dramatic changes of expression. Without the living presence one attends more closely to what is said and how Frost says it. For "narrow views" I would substitute monotonous metrics and a monotony of tone which results from a narrowly calculated vocabulary. In this he resembles Housman or even John Clare; but the resemblance is only superficial. I don't want the old gentleman to turn over in his grave; and yet I must risk it when I agree with Herbert Howarth that Frost was a reformer of poetic diction contemporaneous with Ford Madox Ford, Pound, and Eliot; and that the necessity of reform was as plain to him, even if the result was different, as it was to his younger contemporaries. I shall return to this matter after a personal digression which I hope will be allowed me.

At the end of September 1928 I had arrived in London as a Guggenheim Fellow. I met in the first week a few English writers through the kindness of T. S. Eliot and Herbert Read. I don't remember whether the invitation came from Read or Eliot; at any rate an emissary, Frank Morley, a man my age, came for me in Kensington Garden Square to escort me to my first *Criterion* luncheon at a pub whose name I forget. (After lunch Morley took me on a "pub crawl"—which may explain my faulty memory of that first meeting with Eliot and Read, with whom I had had previous correspondence.) After my second or third *Criterion* luncheon I received an invitation from Harold Monro (whom I had not met) to come to a party at his flat above the famous Poetry Bookshop at 38 Great Russell Street. I do not remember the exact date in October; I don't think it could have been a party given *after* Robert Frost's reading on the 18th at the Poetry Book-shop; nor on the 19th, after Monro had brought Frost and Eliot together at dinner; for at the party I attended there were ten or twelve people present, but not Eliot. I remember vividly Frank Flint—F. S. Flint, the prominent Imagist now forgotten by everybody except literary historians.

Herbert Read soon came to talk to me, and then took me to the other end of the room (near a grate fire) where a circle of men were listening to an animated monologue. The circle broke and I was introduced to "Mr. Robert Frost." He turned to face me and we shook hands. We talked a little, about what I don't remember, but he asked me where I was from; I think I said Kentucky and Virginia. And he said to the company—which included, besides those I have mentioned, A. W. Wheen, Lascelles Abercrombie, Richard Church —he said, "Tate's vowels are different from mine. Just listen. 'The murmurous haunt of flies on summer eves.' Won't you repeat it," he said to me. I did; and he said to the company, "There's the difference between New England and the South." But he then said to me, "Your consonants are too distinct for a Southerner." That's all I remember except the small, sharp eyes, the noble brow, the fine, rugged features, and the dignified bearing. I had read very few of his poems, but I

knew then that I was in the presence of a great man. I didn't
see him again until nineteen years later.

In the commentary that follows—it will be my tribute to
the genius of Robert Frost—I shall try to talk about the
poems I consider the best, regardless of subject or the time
of his life in which they were written. Beginning with *North
of Boston* in 1914 and ending with *In the Clearing* (1962),
when he was eighty-eight, there is a uniformity of style that,
with few exceptions, would make it difficult to date most of
the poems. (*A Boy's Will*, his first book, shows influences,
not of any identifiable poets, but of the period: American
Edwardian or Georgian.) The uniformity of diction has been
called Wordsworthian; but with Frost it is difficult to determine whether theory, as in the case of Wordsworth, or a sure
instinct for what he could best do, explains the monotony of
consciously simplified diction and the prevailing iambic pentameter in both the meditative and the narrative poems. With
the exceptions of the two masques, all his characters talk
alike, with only an occasional departure from the simple but
correct speech of the "literate farmer." One merely observes,
without trying to explain, the comparative inferiority of the
more "lyrical" poems, such as "To Earthward," "An Empty
Threat," "I Will Sing You One, O," and half a dozen others.
One's observation, however, may include the opinion that
Robert Frost was not a first-rate lyric poet, for in this *genre*
he "sings" less than he merely ruminates, as he does at the
end of "To Earthward" or "The Aim Was Song." And the
short political epigrams that he wrote late in life—who will
hold them against him? In more than fifty years of writing
he published about five hundred-sixty poems, some long,
others no more than a few lines. How many did he discard,
unpublished?

No poet so prolific as Robert Frost could expect to write
more good poems than he wrote. Those that I shall comment
on may seem to the Frost devotee an ungenerous, even perverse selection. Are not all the works of the master sacrosanct?

If he has written one great poem, even a very short one, all the others must be considered. To my way of looking at poetry, he wrote more than one great—I shall not say lyric —more than one great short poem, and perhaps a dozen longer pieces. I don't know what else to call the longer poems. They are either meditations or short stories in verse, usually in iambic pentameter and always, whatever the meter and foot, metrical: there is always the tennis net. As to the shorter pieces, he never wrote anything as bad as Shakespeare's Sonnet LXXXV or as great as Sonnet LXXIII; not a bad rating, for those interested in ratings, for any poet since 1616. And although his scene is almost always "country things," I cannot see him with Mr. John F. Lynen as a pastoral poet (*The Pastoral Art of Robert Frost*). I can find neither prelapsarian shepherds nor abstract sheep. There is nothing resembling either the *Idyls* of Theocritus or the *Eclogues* of Vergil. We know that Frost's Latin was fluent, and his Greek adequate, and his command of both languages probably better than Ezra Pound's more ostentatious exhibits. But Frost seems to me to have been too canny to write eclogues and idyls, even though his dialogues may have been suggested by his early reading of Vergil and Theocritus.

Before we pass on from this phase of Frost I should like to look rather closely at what I consider his finest longer— not very long or longest—poem: "The Witch of Coös." A month ago, or a few months hence, I might prefer the shorter "The Wood-Pile" or "West-Running Brook"; for with a poet who wrote so many fine poems choice becomes uncertain and difficult. I am thinking of "The Witch of Coös" because it is typical of Frost's whimsical preference for the shocking circumstance that lies hidden beneath a conventional human situation. Like every first-rate work of art—poem, picture, sculpture, film—it invites endlessly varied interpretations, and all of them may be "right." I wish to look at "The Witch of Coös" through the eyes of Henry James—if I may commit a double presumption, even impertinence. To the question:

what makes the skeleton in the poem fictionally real? there
may be several answers. I assume that everybody knows the
plot, but I shall have to repeat it in outline. The scene is set
in the three opening lines:

> I stayed the night for shelter at a farm
> Behind the mountain, with a mother and son,
> Two old-believers. They did all the talking.

This is not quite plausible: why should the mother tell her
dreadful secret to a stranger, whom the poet makes no effort
to establish as a character? Why did Henry James let the
governess, in *The Turn of the Screw*, write her horrid story
for nobody in particular, although in the Prologue James
explains how her manuscript got into the hands of his host
at an English country house? A fiction must be told to somebody, if it aims at the highest plausibility; otherwise, as in
the primitive novel, the novelist is merely listening to the
sound of his own voice, as Thackeray, a sophisticated Lon-
doner, is doing in his unsophisticated novel *Vanity Fair*. In
"The Witch of Coös," the wayfaring stranger, in the three
lines that I have quoted, not only sets the scene in a remote
place—"behind the mountain"—he tells us that both mother
and son are "old-believers"—hind-sight some time after the
action to prepare us for something, an incident, an unusual
natural phenomenon, or some discredited superstition, to
which he will be the witness. I say "witness" because he not
only hears, he *sees* up to the limit that language will permit
us to see; and it is not fictionally necessary to know whether
this shadowy reporter actually believes what he hears and
sees. But let me dispose at once of the single flaw that I can
find in an otherwise almost perfect work. (I say almost because no work of art is perfect.) It was not at all necessary
to make the mother a spirit-medium, a table-rapper who can
make the table kick "like an army mule." The action begins
when the son asks his mother:

> You wouldn't want to tell him what we have
> Up in the attic?

And she replies:

> Bones—a skeleton.

This "dreadfully" complex poem is, amusingly enough, a
marvelous development of the common saying that we all
have a skeleton in the closet. What appears to have happened
is this: the mother had committed adultery with a man whom
her husband killed, she says, "instead of me." They bury the
corpse in the cellar. Her relation to her husband is frigid.
She says:

> I went to sleep before I went to bed
> Especially in winter when the bed
> Might just as well be ice and the clothes snow.

The bones come up the cellar stairs, "two footsteps for each
step." Her curiosity is so great that she waits for him to
see "how they were mounted for this walk." The skeleton
stretched out its hand and she struck it, breaking off a finger,
which she keeps in her "button box." The common details by
which the bones are made credible are the selection of a
master: we are not allowed to see too much, or even very
much. Frost instinctively found himself among the masters
of credibility for the supernatural: Henry James and W. W.
Jacobs: whether the supernatural be hallucinatory or what
it purports to be need not concern us here.

Let us glance at the way the woman sees the bones (as
she always speaks of them), for that is the way Frost will
let us see them. The "bones" emerge from the cellar; she
sees "them put together./Not like a man, but like a chan-
delier." And then:

> Still going every which way in the joints, though,
> So that it looked like lightning, or a scribble,
> From the slap I had just now given its hand.

She calls upstairs to her husband to get up, and she follows
the bones to their bedroom, where she admits to her husband,
whose curious name is Toffile, that she can't see the bones,
but insisting that they want to go up to the attic, which they
do without being seen by her husband, or seen a second time
by her. Toffile is ordered by his wife to get nails and nail up
the door to the attic where the bones have presumably fled;
and Toffile pushes the headboard of their bed against the
attic door.

> Behind the door and headboard of the bed,
> Brushing their chalky skull with chalky fingers,
> With sounds like the dry rattling of a shutter,
> That's what I sit up in the dark to say—
> To no one anymore since Toffile died.
> Let them stay in the attic since they went there.
> I promised Toffile to be cruel to them
> For helping them be cruel once to him.

The wayfaring stranger has the last word:

> She hadn't found the finger-bone she wanted
> Among the buttons poured out in her lap.
> I verified the name next morning: Toffile.
> The rural letter-box said Toffile Lajway.

James would not have let her find it; nor would Jacobs in
his masterpiece "The Monkey's Paw." You will remember
that great story. The son of an elderly couple is dead, but
they are promised his return from the grave. He does return,
as far as the front door where his parents are waiting to
receive him. But they never see him. The story ends with

the psychic shock resulting from having heard a walking corpse, without actually seeing it. Is the widow a witch because she alone, *when alone*, could see the bones and snatch a finger? There is no indication that she saw them again. Are they merely the "dry rattling of a shutter"? We shall never know; and I submit that Frost's little masterpiece would be ruined if we could know. Canny old Robert might himself have told us that he didn't know. At any rate, what James said in the Preface to *The Aspern Papers* is a rule that Frost's genius knew without James' help. Apparitions, said James, should do as little as is consistent with their consenting to appear at all.

Frost's most popular poems are little short stories in verse, a feature observed by many critics, preeminently by W. W. Robson whose essay in the Autumn 1966 issue of *The Southern Review* seems to me the best short study of Frost that we have. I would amend Robson's perception: short story to anecdote. I would cite a few famous poems that seem to me to be brilliant anecdotes. An anecdote differs from a short story in having a simple plot, or a single incident, in which there is no change of character. Even "The Witch of Coös" is an elaborated anecdote. The most obvious of Robert Frost's anecdotes is "The Death of the Hired Man." (It is not only obvious, it is one of the best of its *genre*.) The old man comes back to work, and he is a skilled hay-pitcher. Warren, the farmer-employer, doesn't want to take him back, but his wife insists. So Warren goes back to the old man, returns to his wife to report him dead; and the poem ends. The anecdote is "used," the old dying hired man is "used," to create a quasi-dramatic situation for two opposing epigrams about the nature of a home. Warren's: "Home is the place where, when you have to go there,/They have to take you in." Mary's: ". . . I should have called it/Something you somehow haven't to deserve."

There is always with us the famous "Birches," a poem that I am fond of with the least possible admiration—the way we sometimes feel about certain old friends. Not that it isn't beautifully written. I don't remember ever mentioning it in print, but I must have written about it long ago, for Mr. Radcliffe Squires says that I consider it an allegory of the poet (*The Major Themes of Robert Frost*, 1963). Poets are like swingers of birches, for they too are engaged upon a profitless enterprise. "That would be good both going and coming back": it is good to write the poem (this is the up-swing), and it is good to see it finished (this is the down-swing). I have felt for a long time that "Marse Robert" might have spared us the sententious meiosis of the last line. Do I need to quote it? I will quote it: "One could do worse than be a swinger of birches." Yes—of course; but unless they are symbolic birches (in an Emersonian direction), if they are just plain birches, one could talk back and say that one could do a lot better than be a swinger of birches. The birches seem too frail to bear such a portentous allegory.

And now the famous wall that has a fine, domestic, and civic effect upon the people it divides. Either wall or fence. Alas, *something* can neither like nor dislike a wall—unless Frost is saying that mystery shrouds the human resistance to con-finement, or perimeters, of any kind; and he observes nature's harsh treatment of walls and fences; the stones must be put up again, year after year, as the two characters in the poem are doing. This is the action to which their dialogue about fences is the accompaniment. Nobody likes walls or fences, but if we are going to live near one another, if we are going to have even the first bare rudiment of a civilized society, we had better do something to preserve the privacy of the family, like putting up a fence or a wall; otherwise we will find ourselves living atavistically in a tribal society. I hope my rather feckless paraphrase of this poem is at least as tiresome as the poem itself. I have a little more to say about it. Good neighbors are good to have, but good fences do not make them good neighbors. Here we have Frost's perilous teetering upon the brink of sentimentality. Fences good or bad make nothing; but upon the rhetorical trick that attributes causation to them the poem depends. I could wish that this fine poet had drawn upon his classical learning and had alluded to the first thing the Romans did when they were making a settlement: they built a low wall that would enclose a forum and in the middle set up an altar. The wall around the altar shut out the Infinite, or as the Greeks said it, τὸ ἄπειρον, as if they might have foreseen the disorderly love of infinity that Walt Whitman would bring into the world. May I suggest that Frost's limited perspective in this poem is due to what I have called (after Samuel Johnson) his "narrow views"? The views are not only opinions but the deliberate restriction of his language to the range possible to that ghostly, hypothetical person, the "literate farmer." Short range of consciousness means limited diction. I shall have more to say about this in a moment.

I cannot do much about a list of very fine poems which there is no time to discuss in detail. "The White-Tailed Hornet," "Place for a Third," "A Star in a Stone Boat," "Two Tramps in Mud Time," "Fear," "Once by the Pacific," "After Apple-Picking." One tires of making lists. Tomorrow I might make another list, equally distinguished, attaching to it a list of neutral poems that exhibit the defect of Frost's quality. So I shall now indulge in what will look like a digression, and may actually be a digression which was suggested by Mr. Howarth's valuable essay in the Frost symposium in the Autumn 1966 issue of *The Southern Review.* He is, I believe, the only critic to see in Frost's restricted diction a revolutionary reform contemporaneous with the experiments in poetic diction of Pound and Eliot. Pound, in England, was Frost's first champion; but Frost would not follow Pound into an international, eclectic, and "learned" style. (Is this the meaning of Frost's "The Road Not Taken"? Perhaps.) At any rate Frost must have believed that in order to break new stylistic ground he had to *locate it literally.* It was inevitable that he would locate it in New England. Half

Scottish, half New Englander, he was taken by his widowed mother from San Francisco to New England when he was eleven. He had the ideal upbringing for a poet, and it is irrelevant that he disliked it. He was half in and half out, and he could take nothing for granted; thus his powers of observation, which were great, led to equally great gifts for discovery: he saw New England nature and the nature of New England man as his own, but both natures had to be discovered. He therefore invented a language for this double imaginative activity. He was much more the conscious technician than some of his critics have thought. Did he not write to his friend John Bartlett that he was one of the great craftsmen? There is nothing reprehensible in this kind of boasting if it is true; and this was.

For many years I have argued with skeptics that the Eliot-Pound revolution was as radical as that brought about by two other young men in 1798—or rather by one of them, William Wordsworth. In the famous Preface to the 1800 edition of *Lyrical Ballads* Wordsworth said that he wanted to write in the "real language of men." Which men? Rural men was the answer, and he wrote a masterpiece called "Michael." But Frost's "literate farmer" never gave utterance to such absurdities as "Peter Bell" and "The Idiot Boy"; nor did he ever, as Mr. Robson points out, achieve the grandeur of "Resolution and Independence." Wordsworth broke out of his early mold; Robert Frost did not. Yet in certain respects Frost was subtler and a more sensitive listener to the sounds of poetry. He anticipated by many years T. S. Eliot's discovery of the "auditory imagination." Frost called it the audile (or audial) imagination, and he described it as the "sound of the meaning"—a very different effect from that which Pope had in mind when he wrote that "the sound must seem to echo in the sense." I take it that Frost would have said that there is no meaning to be sounded in a line like "The Hounds of Spring are on winter's traces," etc.

As I approach the end of these scattered observations I

allude to three or four poems that seem to me Robert Frost's best: "The Wood-Pile," which ends with the great line "With the slow smokeless burning of decay"; "After Apple Picking"; "The Onset"; and "The Oven Bird." But where is "Stopping by Woods on a Snowy Evening"? Had Frost written this one short masterpiece and no others, his name would last as long as poetry itself will last. (We cannot assume that even poetry will last forever.) Here it is:

> Whose woods these are I think I know.
> His house is in the village, though,
> He will not see me stopping here
> To watch his woods fill up with snow.
>
> My little horse may think it queer
> To stop without a farmhouse near
> Between the woods and frozen lake
> The darkest evening of the year.
>
> He gives his harness bells a shake
> To ask if there is some mistake.
> The only other sound's the sweep
> Of easy wind and downy flake.
>
> The woods are lovely, dark and deep,
> But I have promises to keep,
> And miles to go before I sleep,
> And miles to go before I sleep.

It has the rhyme scheme of Fitzgerald's *Rubaiyat* stanza: *a a b a.* But the meter is tetrameter, not as in the *Rubaiyat,* pentameter. The four stanzas are "linked" in much the same way as Dante's *terzine* are linked. The unrhymed "here" in the first stanza is rhymed with the two first lines and with the fourth of the second; and so on, until we get to the last stanza, in which the third line rhymes with two and four; in short, one rhyme only in that stanza, as one will repeat a phrase, or see oneself walking in a dream, or as one drifts off into sleep. These formalistic external features of the poem have scarcely been noticed; they contribute to the overwhelming, if quiet, effect. Here our literate farmer is, in the very first line, highly sophisticated: it contains both a question and the answer to the question: Whose woods are these? And in the same grammatical sequence: I think I know. But the owner is in town, and he will not see me observe the recurrent mystery of winter, which is snow. We are not told that the man watching the snowfall is in a sleigh: the horse knows that something unusual is happening, though not to the eye, his or his master's. There is no house nearby: the man is isolated in the "darkest evening," his own darkness. The "harness bells" add a dimension of sound to the sibilance of the blowing snow. The lake is frozen: the usually beneficent water is obdurate, and nature has withdrawn her protection. The fourth stanza has all the appearance of the calculation of genius.

But Frost told a friend that the entire poem came to him in a flash, or rather phrase by phrase, rhyme-scheme and meter, without a pause. There is every reason to believe him. The external pattern reflects perfectly what we are told; instead of the third unrhymed line, as in the three other stanzas, there is, as I have said, one rhyme: deep-keep-sleep-sleep. As one falls asleep it takes too much effort to find a rhyme; so sleep echoes sleep. We may see here what Mr. Cleanth Brooks formerly saw as a paradox: the poet falls asleep as he tells us that he will not. But the most brilliant single word in the poem is that common word "lovely." Years ago I almost dismissed the poem because "lovely" struck me as a lazy evasion of the precise word. But it *is* the precise word. The woods are a lovely woman, but a woman cold, mysterious (dark), and unfathomable: and he must not succumb to this temptress, who is both life and death. Frost thought of the poem as a "death poem." As I see it, it has as much of life in it as any poem of the same length in the language. It could hold its own with the great lyric of the nineteenth century, "Tears, Idle Tears."

In the spring of 1961 Robert Frost came to Minneapolis to give a reading at the University of Minnesota. I was asked to introduce him, which I took great pleasure in doing, to a packed auditorium of five thousand persons. He was the house-guest of a colleague of mine, Charles Foster, a former student of Frost's at Amherst. Frost was with us almost a week. I had two parties for him. At the second party, at about two in the morning, after all the guests except the Fosters had gone home, he asked for another brandy. I brought it to him, though I could hardly stand up, not from intoxication but from fatigue. He was then eighty-seven.

On January 5, 1963, I was at Yale, in the library, as a member of the jury for the Bollingen Prize of 1962. Up to that time the Bollingen juries tacitly assumed that to award Robert Frost the prize would carry coals to Newcastle. But in 1963 we knew he was dying in a Boston hospital. There was no time left for him to get the Nobel Prize. The jury— composed of Robert Lowell, John Hall Wheelock, Richard Eberhart, the late Louise Bogan, and myself, voted unanimously to award him the prize. Would he accept it? I was appointed to telephone him and ask. I did; his feeble voice came through distinctly. "Is this Allen?" he said. I said, "Yes, and we hope you will accept the Bollingen Prize for 1962." After a brief silence he said, "I've wondered where you fellows stood."

Introduction to *White Buildings*
by Hart Crane

1926

T HE POETRY of Hart Crane is ambitious. It is the only poetry I am acquainted with which is at once contemporary and in the grand manner. It is an American poetry. Crane's themes are abstractly, metaphysically conceived, but they are definitely confined to an experience of the American scene. In such poems as "The Wine Menageries," "For the Marriage of Faustus and Helen," "Recitative," he is the poet of the complex urban civilization of his age: precision, abstraction, power. There is no *pastiche*; when he employs symbols from traditional literature, the intention is personally symbolic; it is never falsely pretentious with the common baggage of poetical speech.

Hart Crane's first experiments in verse are not, of course, collected in this volume, which contains, with one or two exceptions, only those poems exhibiting the qualities likely to be permanent in his work. Of these exceptions there is the perfectly written piece of Imagism, "Garden Abstract." This poem evinces several properties of the "new poetry" of a decade ago, the merits and the limitations of the Imagists.

To the Imagists Crane doubtless went to school in poetry. He learned their structural economy; he followed their rejection of the worn-out poetic phrase; he must have studied the experiments in rhythm of Pound, Aldington, Fletcher. From Pound and Eliot he got his first conception of what it is, in the complete sense, to be contemporary.

But Crane suddenly and profoundly broke with the methods of Imagism, with its decorative and fragmentary world. To the conceptual mind a world set up not by inclusive assertion but by exclusive attention to the objects of sense lacks imaginative coordination; a method which refuses to exceed the dry presentation of *petites sensations* confines the creative vision to suggestions, to implicit indications, but it cannot arrive at the direct affirmation, of a complete world. A series of Imagistic poems is a series of worlds. The poems of Hart Crane are facets of a single vision; they refer to a central imagination, a single evaluating power, which is at once the motive of the poetry and the form of its realization.

The poet who tries to release the imagination as an integer of perception attempts the solution of the leading contemporary problem of his art. It would be impertinent to enumerate here the underlying causes of the dissociation of the modern consciousness: the poet no longer apprehends his world as a whole. The dissociation appears decisively for the first time in Baudelaire. It is the separation of vision and subject; since Baudelaire's time poets have in some sense been deficient in the one or the other. For the revolt of Rimbaud, in this distinction, was a repudiation of the commonly available themes of poetry, followed by a steady attenuation of vision in the absence of thematic control. Exactly to the extent to which the ready-made theme controls the vision, the vision is restricted by tradition and may, to that extent, be defined by tradition. In *The Waste Land*, which revives the essence of the problem, Mr. Eliot displays vision and subject once more in traditional schemes; the vision for some reason is dissipated, and the subject dead. For while Mr. Eliot might have written a more ambitiously unified poem, the unity would have been false; tradition as unity is not contemporary. The important contemporary poet has the rapidly diminishing privilege of reorganizing the subjects of the past. He must construct and assimilate his own subjects. Dante had only to assimilate his.

If the energy of Crane's vision never quite reaches a sustained maximum, it is because he has not found a suitable theme. To realize even partially, at the present time, the maximum of poetic energy demonstrates an important intention. Crane's poems are a fresh vision of the world, so intensely personalized in a new creative language that only the strictest and most unprepossessed effort of attention can take it in. Until vision and subject completely fuse, the poems will be difficult. The comprehensiveness and lucidity of any poetry are in direct proportion to the availability of a comprehensive and perfectly articulated given theme.

Crane wields a sonorous rhetoric that takes the reader to Marlowe and the Elizabethans. His blank verse, the most sustained medium he controls, is pre-Websterian; it is measured, richly textured, rhetorical. But his spiritual allegiances are outside the English tradition. Melville and Whitman are his avowed masters. In his sea poems, "Voyages," in "Emblems of Conduct," in allusions to the sea throughout his work, there is something of Melville's intense, transcendental brooding on the mystery of the "high interiors of the sea." I do not know whether he has mastered Poe's criticism, yet some of his conviction that the poet should be intensely local must stem from Poe. Most of it, however, he undoubtedly gets from Whitman. Whitman's range was possible in an America of prophecy; Crane's America is materially the same, but it approaches a balance of forces; it is a realization; and the poet, confronted with a complex present experience, gains in intensity what he loses in range. The great proportions of the myth have collapsed in its reality. Crane's poetry is a concentration of certain phases of the Whitman substance, the fragments of the myth.

The great difficulty which his poetry presents the reader is the style. It is possible that his style may check the immediate currency of the most distinguished American poetry of the age, for there has been very little preparation in America for a difficult poetry; the Imagistic impressionism of the last ten years has not supplied it. Although Crane is probably not a critical and systematic reader of foreign literatures, his French is better than Whitman's; he may have learned something from Laforgue and, particularly, Rimbaud; or something of these poets from Miss Sitwell, Mr. Wallace Stevens, or Mr. T. S. Eliot.

He shares with Rimbaud the device of oblique presentation of theme. The theme never appears in explicit statement. It is formulated through a series of complex metaphors which defy a paraphrasing of the sense into an equivalent prose. The reader is plunged into a strangely unfamiliar *milieu* of sensation, and the principle of its organization is not immediately grasped. The *logical* meaning can never be derived (see "Passage," "Lachrymae Christi"); but the *poetical* meaning is a direct intuition, realized prior to an explicit knowledge of the subject-matter of the poem. The poem does not *convey*; it *presents*; it is not topical, but expressive.

There is the opinion abroad that Crane's poetry is, in some indefinite sense, "new." It is likely to be appropriated by one of the several esoteric cults of the American soul. It tends toward the formation of a state of mind, the critical equivalent of which would be in effect an exposure of the confusion and irrelevance of the current journalism of poetry, and of how far behind the creative impulse the critical intelligence, at the moment, lags. It is to be hoped, therefore, that this state of mind, where it may be registered at all, will not at its outset be shunted into a false context of obscure religious values, that a barrier will not be erected between it and the rational order of criticism. For, unless the present critic is deceived as to the structure of his tradition, the well-meaning criticism since Poe has supported a vicious confusion: it has transferred the states of mind of poetry from their proper contexts to the alien contexts of moral and social aspiration. The moral emphasis is valid; but its focus on the consequences of the state of mind, instead of on its properties as art, has throttled a tradition in poetry. The moral values of literature should derive from literature, not from the personal values of the critic; their public circulation in criticism, if they are not ultimately to be rendered inimical to literature, should be controlled by the literary intention. There have been poetries of "genius" in America, but each of these as poetry has been scattered, and converted into an *impasse* to further extensions of the same order of imagination.

A living art is new; it is old. The formula which I have contrived in elucidation of Crane's difficulty for the reader (a thankless task, since the difficulty inheres equally in him) is a formula for most romantic poetry. Shelley could not have been influenced by Rimbaud, but he wrote this "difficult" verse:

> Pinnacled dim in the intense inane.

The present faults of Crane's poetry (it has its faults: it is not the purpose of this foreword to disguise them) cannot be isolated in a line-by-line recognition of his difficulty. If the poems are sometimes obscure, the obscurity is structural and deeper. His faults, as I have indicated, lie in the occasional failure of meeting between vision and subject. The vision often strains and overreaches the theme. This fault, common among ambitious poets since Baudelaire, is not unique with them. It appears whenever the existing poetic order no longer supports the imagination. It appeared in the eighteenth century with the poetry of William Blake.

The Poetry of Edgar Allan Poe

1968

IN 1948 T. S. ELIOT, in a lecture "From Poe to Valéry,"
said in substance that Poe's work, if it is to be judged
fairly, must be seen as a whole, lest as the mere sum of
its parts it seem inferior. There is much truth in this; but it
puts an unusual strain upon the critic. I believe that I have
read, over many years, everything that Poe wrote, but I have
never been aware of it all at any one time; nor am I now, as
I approach a discussion of the poems. Do the poems increase
or diminish one's sense of Poe's greatness if considered apart
from the prose, as if the prose did not exist? European critical
practice would forbid such a separation, and would compel us
to see the poems as one expression of a complex personality
responding to the undeveloped society of the New World.
This would have been Taine's "method" and, later in the
nineteenth century, the method of Georg Brandes. These
critic-historians frequently produced elaborate commentaries
and "explanations" of an author more interesting than the
works of the author himself. That has not been an achievement of modern American criticism. We worry the single
poem almost to death; we substitute what Poe himself called

Introduction to the New American Library edition of *The Complete Poems and Selected Criticism of Edgar Allan Poe.*

"analysis" for "passion"; yet the results have been on the whole rewarding, in that large numbers of persons who never read poetry before have learned how to read it and enjoy it. And we have developed more than any other age a criticism of criticism. But we have not done so well with the larger works like the novel, or even the *nouvelle*. We do not see the larger works, nor the collected works, of an author as a whole.

I shall therefore try to "introduce" readers to the poetry of Edgar Allan Poe as I myself was introduced to it in boyhood, when I read almost anything out of curiosity; that is to say, Poe was in the house and I read him as I read the Rover Boys. But the difference, which appeared only much later, was that I retained Poe, whereas the Rover Boys, Tom Swift, and G. A. Henty soon became a blank; of this sort of author I remember only that Tom Swift had an electric rifle. There was, of course, Natty Bumppo; but he was not, any more than Tom, a book, but a character of the mythical order of George Washington, different, but not literature. One does not know, at the age of fourteen, that there is such a thing as literature; but at or at about that age I remember finding somewhere on a top shelf in the dingy parlor three small volumes of Edgar Allan Poe. They may have been part of the infamous Griswold edition; at any rate they were not the complete works. One volume contained some of the more famous tales, as well as the stories of ratiocination, like "The Murders in the Rue Morgue" and "The Mystery of Marie Rogêt." These stories gave the adolescent mind the illusion of analytical thought. Some of the others, such as "The Premature Burial" and "The Facts in the Case of M. Valdemar," raised questions that seemed at fourteen the deepest inquiries possible into the relation of body and soul: pseudo-philosophy for the unformed and ignorant mind. How a child's reading of Poe's prose tales affected his reading of the poems I shall try to explain, or at least to describe, in a moment.

One of the three volumes contained *Eureka*—the work, in fact, took up the entire book—and it was the first essay in

cosmology that I read. It led just a little later to Ernst
Haeckel's *The Riddle of the Universe*, the crassest materialis-
tic cosmogony produced in the nineteenth century, and then
to Herbert Spencer's *Synthetic Philosophy*. But *Eureka* is
the only piece of adolescent reading in popular astronomy to
which I have returned in age; and I still take it seriously. I
have wondered why the modern proponents of the Big Bang
hypothesis of the creation have not condescended to acknowledge Poe as a forerunner. Big Bang presupposes an agent
to set off the explosion of the primordial atom; and that is
what Poe presupposed in his fundamental thesis for *Eureka*:
"In the original unity of the first thing lies the secondary
cause of all things, with the germ of their inevitable annihilation." But the concluding phrase presupposes something else,
which is characteristic of Poe in all phases of his work: "inevitable annihilation." The cosmos will shrink back into
spatial nothingness, taking man along with it; and hence man,
having returned to the original nothing, which is God, will *be*
God. The last twenty or so pages of *Eureka* have a lurid,
rhetorical magnificence unmatched by anything else that Poe
wrote. For *Eureka* is Poe's elaborate, pseudo-systematic attempt to give his compulsive theme of annihilation scientific
and philosophical sanctions.

The theme of annihilation is always attractive to young
persons: from about twelve to sixteen, annihilation or simply
romantic death at the end of sentimental love—an adolescent
posture of disorder set against the imposed order of the family
or of adult society into which the child resists entrance. This
posture of disorder is never quite rejected in maturity, and it
is the psychological and moral basis of what today is called
existentialism. One reason why Americans may be a little
bored with French existentialism is that we have always been
existentialists, or have been since the time of Poe, who discovered it in us. For existentialism assumes—among other
things—that man has no relation to a metaphysical reality,
a kind of reality that he cannot know even if it existed; he is

therefore trapped in a consciousness which cannot be conscious of anything outside itself. He must sink into the non-self. Poe sinks into the vortex, the maelstrom, suffocation of premature burial or of being walled up alive; or he sinks into the sea. We know Coleridge's influence on Poe. How apt for Poe's purposes was the "lifeless ocean" of Coleridge! And the death of a beautiful woman was, for Poe, the most "poetical" subject for poetry—or, as we should say today, the archetypal subject. One of his best lyrics begins, "Thou wast that all to me, Love,/For which my soul did pine. . . ." His love is dead, of course, and he is left *alone,* ready for loss of breath, loss of consciousness, loss of identity—*never more* anything outside himself. I shall have something to say presently about the Raven's "Nevermore." I must end these preliminary observations with some attention to the word *alone.*

Among the poems attributed to Poe, the authorship of which cannot be proved, is a piece entitled "Alone"; yet what the scholars call "internal evidence" is so obvious that I do not hesitate to use it as a key to some of his compulsive symbols which are ultimately, as I have indicated, a single symbolic matrix: the vortex, the grave, the pit. Here I quote the significant lines:

> From childhood's hour I have not been
> As others were—
> . . . I could not awaken
> My heart to joy at the same tone;
> And all I lov'd *I* lov'd alone.
> *Then*—in my childhood—in the dawn
> Of a most stormy life—was drawn
> From ev'ry depth of good and ill
> The mystery which binds me still. . .
> From the thunder and the storm,
> And the cloud that took the form
> (When the rest of Heaven was blue)
> Of a demon in my view.

The poem, first published in 1875, was found in an autograph album belonging to a lady in Baltimore; it was the opinion of the late Killis Campbell that the poem was written as early as 1829 or 1830, when Poe was not older than twenty-one. (I pause to observe that four-fifths of Poe's poems, however many times he reprinted them, often in versions revised almost beyond recognition, were written by the time he was twenty-two.) Yet one might guess from the tone of the poem that it was written in retrospect, towards the end of a long life. At twenty-one his childhood was not in the remote past. What kind of demon was it that Poe saw in his childhood— or saw when he was writing the poem, which comes to the same thing? Elsewhere I have called Poe a forlorn demon gazing at himself in a glass; thus could William Wilson be described, and likewise most of Poe's fictional heroes. I suggest that Poe's poetry, which consists of only some sixty-odd authenticated poems, most of them very short, were all written by Poe as his own fictional projection; by Poe as the demon he tells us he saw take shape in a cloud.

There is nothing very shocking about this. A non-theological view of demonology would tell us that a demon is simply a person who cannot develop—a fierce determinism has arrested the rounded growth of his faculties, so that the evil he does other persons is not a positive malice but an insistence that they remain as emotionally and intellectually deprived as he himself must remain. Poe's poems, from first to last, from "Tamerlane" to "Ulalume," show almost no change, certainly no acquisition of range and depth that might justly be described as development. All of his poems might have been written in any one year of his life, at age fifteen or age forty (his age when he died); that most of them were written before 1831 was probably due to the later financial necessity of making a living out of literary journalism. (He was the first committed and perhaps still the greatest American literary journalist on the high French model: a critical tradition represented today by Edmund Wilson and Malcolm Cowley.)

In the short introduction to *Eureka* he said that poetry with him had been a "passion," leaving the implication that he had had no time to write much of it. One may reasonably doubt the validity of this explanation, though one may not doubt Poe's sincerity in thinking it valid. He had enough time from 1831 to his death in 1849 to rewrite most of the poems, some of them many times. I think it is fair to infer from all the evidence that he had very little, or rather one thing, to say in poetry; in the revisions he was trying to say it better or was trying, by means of deletions and additions, to make old poems look like new poems—for what reason one may only guess: perhaps to sell the same but disguised poem several times, perhaps to keep his "image" as a poet before the public, or perhaps, as I have indicated, to improve the poems.

The one thing he had to say I have briefly indicated; but before I develop the theme in a scrutiny of some of the best poems I shall glance at his life. More than any other romantic poet, here or in England, either of the preceding generation of Coleridge, Wordsworth, and Bryant, or of his own, he became the *type*, not the greatest but the most representative: that is to say, he became the *type* of the alienated poet, the outcast, the *poète maudit*—the poet accursed. I hope I am not pushing this matter too far if I see in "Alone" his early awareness of his plight. The demon-cloud had early uttered its malediction. N. Bryllion Fagin tells us about the "histrionic Mr. Poe," and quite justly. Yet the self-conscious dramatization of doom, fully developed towards the end of his life in "The Raven" and "Ulalume," was not consciously assumed as a pose; it came from the inside, out of his early life; and I can think of no other writer of the nineteenth century who was more entitled to a conviction of his doom (if anybody ever is) than Edgar Allan Poe. The doom, then, was sincere, if consciously exploited.

Why was Poe entitled to it? He had the "education of a gentleman," five years as a boy in England and a few months at the University of Virginia, financed by a foster-father who never legally adopted the boy and who rejected him when his protector died. The protector was the first Mrs. John Allan. The second Mrs. Allan did not like Poe, whose gambling debts at the university gave Allan an excuse for cutting him off. Professor Arthur Hobson Quinn makes it plain that another reason, perhaps the decisive one, was Poe's knowledge of John Allan's mistress and his illegitimate children, which brought on the final quarrel. Poe was not prepared for any of the three respectable vocations of the Old South: the law, the army, and the Church. A classically educated man in Virginia who had neither a vocation nor landed property could not have a place in the Southern social scheme. At twenty Poe was a gentleman without family, property, or vocation; so he enlisted in the army under the name of Edgar A. Perry. From then on, though he soon reclaimed his name, he lived what was virtually an anonymous life, a professional writer in a country that did not recognize letters as a profession. If history had consciously set about creating the character and circumstances favorable to the appearance of the archetype of the romantic poet, it could not have done better than to select Poe for the role and Richmond as the place for his appearance.

The pure romantic poet, either through choice (Shelley) or through circumstance (Poe), or partly one, partly the other (Keats), must isolate himself, or be isolated, or simply find himself isolated for the deeply felt but not consciously known purposes of his genius. He must, in short, be *alone*.

A poet may have many subjects, but few poets since the the time of Blake have had more than one theme; such poets must try again and again to give the theme, in successive poems, new and if possible fuller expression. One might see the relation of theme to subject as a relation of potency to actualization. The romantic poet is trying to write one poem all his life, out of an interior compulsion; each poem is an approximation of the Perfect Romantic Poem. I do not wish to be understood as saying that the Romantic Poet is the polar opposite of the Classical Poet, or that there are generic differences which point to distinct categories of poetry. A poet like Ben Jonson has many themes but only one style; Poe has one theme and many styles, or many approximations of one style, none of them perfect, and some very bad, as we shall presently see.

There are four poems by Poe that I believe everybody can join in admiring: "The City in the Sea," "The Sleeper," "To Helen" (the shorter and earlier poem of that title), and "The Raven"; one might include "Ulalume," but less as distinguished poetry than as Poe's last and most ambitious attempt to actualize in language his *aloneness*.

"To Helen" is somewhat more complex than the critics have found it to be, or found it necessary to point out. However, the similarity to Landor has been frequently remarked, but nobody knows whether the influence was direct. (Whether the poem was addressed to an older lady who was kind to Poe when he was a boy is irrelevant.) The direct address is to "Helen," inevitably Helen of Troy whether or not Poe had her in mind; and the tact with which she is described is Homeric. She is not *described* at all; she is presented in a long simile of action, in which her beauty is conveyed to the reader through its effect on the speaker of the poem. There is nothing else in Poe's work quite so well done as this.

In the second stanza one might detect a small blemish (the poem is so nearly perfect that it invites close scrutiny): the phrase "thy Naiad airs" might be better if the noun were in the singular—"thy Naiad *air*," meaning that her demeanor or bearing is that of a Naiad; the plural has a slight connotation of the colloquial "putting on airs." Helen brings the wanderer home to his native shore, which is the ancient world: the Landoresque perfection of the two last lines of the second stanza has not been surpassed. But the complexity of feeling, unusual in Poe, comes in the last stanza with the image of Helen as a statue in a niche, perhaps at the end of a hall, or on a landing of a stairway. She has all along been both the disturbing Helen and, as a marble, a Vestal Virgin holding her lamp: she is inaccessible. The restrained exclamation "Ah, Psyche" is one of the most brilliant effects in romantic poetry. "Ah" has the force of "alas": alas, that Helen is now in a lost, if holy land, as inaccessible and pure as she herself is. But who is Psyche? She is usually identified with Helen, and she may be Helen, but at the same time she is the Psyche of Eros and Psyche· and Poe must have known the little myth in Appuleius: she could be an archetype of suprasensual love by means of which the classical, sensual Helen is sublimated. (In "Ulalume" Psyche appears again, as the sister of the poet.) Poe wrote the poem when he was not more than twenty-one; he pretended to Lowell that he had written it when he was fourteen; but whenever he wrote it he never before nor afterwards had such mastery of diction and rhythm. I need not point out that the theme of the poem is isolation of the poet after great loss.

Poe's aesthetic theory has not been overrated, but it has been complicated by certain scholars who have tried to show that the theory implies systematic thought; he was, on the contrary, not a systematic critical thinker but a practical critic who on the whole was limited by the demands of book-reviewing, by which he made a great part of his living. The essay most popular in his time was "The Poetic Principle," actually a lecture, what we know today as a "poetry reading with commentary." Poe was the first itinerant American poet who thus became known to hundreds of people who never read a line of his writing. The "Letter to Mr. B.," written when he was about twenty, is a simplified theft from Chapter XIV of *Biographia Literaria*. His review of Hawthorne states brilliantly the necessity for organic unity in fiction, a principle applicable also to poetry. His theory of prosody, which he developed in "The Rationale of Verse," founders on a misconception of the *caesura*.

In the long run his theory of poetry is quite simple: "the

rhythmical creation of Beauty" is the end of poetry, which is most completely realized in that most poetical of subjects, the death of a beautiful woman, or more often, in his own verse, the beautiful woman's corpse. He derived his psychology from his intellectual climate: Intellect-Feeling-Will. Since the aim of poetry is pleasure, not instruction, both intellect and will are eliminated, and emotion is the limited province of poetry. Poe was the first romantic expressionist in this country: the poet must not think in his poetry; he could be allowed to think only of the means by which the emotionally unthinking subject-matter reaches the reader as an *effect*. The intellect thus operates in technique but not in the poem itself.

It has not been pointed out by the biographers and critics that, although Poe attacked the genteel preaching of Longfellow and Lowell as the "heresy of the didactic," he was himself paradoxically a didactic poet, a grim and powerful one at that. He is constantly telling us that we are all alone, that beauty is evanescent, that the only immortality may be a vampirish return from the grave, into which we must sink again through eternity. In "The Haunted Palace" we are taught that the intellect cannot know either nature or other persons. In "The Conqueror Worm," we are taught that life is a "drama" in which we think we are the protagonists; but the actual hero is death in the guise of a gigantic Worm. This is the human "plot." If, as Poe says in *Eureka*, "the universe is a plot of God," and man participates in the plot as a conscious actor, then the purposeless activity of man has as its goal the horror of death and bodily corruption.

It is no wonder, then, that Poe wrote so few poems. There are not many ways to deliver his message of spiritual solipsism and physical decay if the poet limits himself to romantic expressionism. The "rhythmical creation of Beauty" means very little, if anything, as a general aesthetic principle; it means in Poe's poetry the expression of a Pure Emotion which creates in the reader a pure emotional effect, about which we must not think, and about which we must do nothing.

Of the poems which I have mentioned as being among his best, there is no need to discuss at length "The Sleeper," which many critics consider a masterpiece. There is bad writing in it—"The lily lolls upon the wave"; "And this all solemn silentness"—yet it remains Poe's best treatment of the beautiful female corpse. The "lady" will be taken to a vault where her ancestors lie, against which she had "thrown,/In childhood, many an idle stone." This is the only poem in which the dead lady has any life before her appearance on the "bier" or in the tomb. We can almost believe that she was at some remote time a human being; yet why at the end we are told that she was a "child of sin" I cannot discover.

If Poe wrote any "great" poems they are surely "The City in the Sea" and "The Raven."

"The City in the Sea" was first published in 1831 as "The Doomed City"; revised and republished in 1836 as "The City of Sin"; "The City in the Sea" is the title in the 1845 edition of the poems. The recurrent symbolism of the vortex that one finds everywhere in the prose tales appears infrequently and incompletely in the poems; but here it receives its most powerful expression in verse. The nineteenth-century critics—Edmund Clarence Stedman, for example—thought the poem a masterpiece; Edwin Markham put it beside "Kubla Khan." But there is nowhere in the poem evidence of Coleridge's magisterial certainty and control. In the first five lines there is a doggerel movement—"Where the good and the bad and the worst and the best/Have gone to their eternal rest." I have written elsewhere that "everything in Poe is dead"; in this poem everything is dead; for the poem might be entitled "The City of Death." Here we go beyond the lovely dead woman to dead humanity; and all nature, as well, is dead. When this dead city slides into the sea we, presumably, go down with it into the vortex: into oblivion. This archetype of life after death is as old as recorded humanity. In Dante the sea to which we return is the will of God; in Poe it is a dire apocalyptic vision in which we suffer "inevitable annihilation." Except

for "To Helen" the poem contains the best lines Poe ever
wrote:

> But light from out the lurid sea
> Streams up the turrets silently. . . .
> Up many and many a marvellous shrine
> Whose wreathèd friezes intertwine
> The viol, the violet, and the vine.

Ernest Dowson thought the last line the best in English poetry, and T. S. Eliot seemed so charmed by the labio-dental
v's that he let the "nightingale fill all the desert with inviolable
voice." Perhaps Baudelaire imitated

> Down, down that town will settle hence

in the climactic line of *Femmes Damnées*:

> Descendez, descendez, lamentables victimes.

In conclusion I can add very little to the criticism of "The
Raven," a poem so badly, even vulgarly, written in many passages that one wonders how it can be a great poem, which I believe it to be. We have here the two necessary elements—the
beautiful, dead, "lost Lenore" and the *poète maudit* who with
perfect literary tact is confronted with, I dare say, the demon
of the youthful poem "Alone." It is the same demon, this time
come down from the clouds and taking the form of a bird that
imitates human speech without knowing what the speech
means:

> And his eyes have all the seeming of a demon's that
>   is dreaming. . . .

This poem—a late poem, written in 1844—is the one poem by
Poe which is not direct lyrical, or romantic, expressionism. It

has dramatic form and progression: the poet conducts a dialogue with his demon; it is the only poem by Poe which leads the reader through an action. In classical terms, the plot is simple, not complex; it is a simple plot of Recognition in which the poet, examining all the implications of the bird's "Nevermore," recognizes his doom.

Henry James said that admiration of Poe represented a "primitive stage of reflection." One agrees; but one must add that without primitive reflection, however one defines it, one cannot move on.

A Note on Paul Valéry
1970

I N 1932 I WAS in France for the second time, and I hoped
to accomplish what I had failed to do on my first visit four
years earlier: an introduction to Paul Valéry. I had met,
in 1928, through the kind offices of Sylvia Beach, Valéry Larbaud; and now, in 1932, I was reading a small book, just out a
year, by Larbaud, entitled *Fauteuil XXXVIII Paul Valéry*.
Larbaud's essay—it is only some twelve thousand words—was
my first view of Valéry's early life and career; and I still think,
having looked at it again after almost forty years, that it is
perhaps the best brief introduction to Paul Valéry for the foreign reader. The greater part of the book, following Larbaud's
essay, is composed of "Pages Inédites" by Valéry himself. At
that time I had read about a dozen of the poems, including the
four masterpieces, but I had not read any of the essays and
dialogues. "Pages Inédites" is a miscellany of short discourses,
aphorisms, and epigrams in a tradition that was not unknown
to me. I had read in and around the "Pensées" of Pascal;
Valéry was in that tradition, which only the precision of the
French language could have made possible: the formally bal-
anced, elegant *aperçu* tossed off with an air of spontaneity

concealing the hard labor of calculated thought.

I never met Valéry: I cannot remember what went wrong—whether a conflicting engagement prevented Larbaud from taking me to see him, or whether it was Julien Green who had promised to take me but at the last minute couldn't. It was just as well: the hero-worship to which I was still susceptible might have clouded, for a few years, the image of the *man in the work;* and it is the work that, in order to be contemporary, must never become wholly contemporaneous. Here, in "Pages Inédites," was a man educated in the French classical tradition and fired imaginatively by his early *entretiens* with Mallarmé; whose apparently casual utterances gave me something more than the shock of recognition. It was rather a sense of my own identity, of a sameness within vast, elusive differences. Two of the *aperçus* I have never forgotten, and I quote them here because to my mind they contain the essence of the elaborate, complex, and subtle speculations that Valéry from time to time issued to relieve the tedium of creative paralysis.

L'intuition sans l'intelligence est un accident.

Les belles oeuvres sont filles de leur forme, qui
NAIT AVANT ELLES.

These opinions—so easily and so gracefully tossed off—have inexhaustible implications which Valéry in his fifty-odd years of intermittent speculation, and even less frequent experiments in verse, was trying to define ever more precisely, not only in poetry (they contain his entire poetics), but in his essays and dialogues: the relation of intelligence and form is the underlying subject of the "Introduction à la méthode de Léonard de Vinci," his first ambitious work, published in 1895.

The scope of this discussion will not allow me to notice, with anything like justice to their merit, the vast number of prose works dealing with the role of the intellect (or of *method,* as Valéry was trying all his life to understand it) in the creative process. The typical Valérian irony of the claim to ignorance in the numerous little essays on painters—Degas, Morisot, Manet—might trap us into thinking that he was better qualified to understand the philosophical or scientific mind, since most of his prose is concerned with *ideas*. But we must not be misled; the irony I have noted is perhaps a little disingenuous intellectually, for there is no reason to believe that Valéry knew more about mathematics than about painting. It was simply that what little he knew he could *use* with greater precision than he could bring to bear upon the problem of form in painting. This is true of the twelve-year-old boy, who to the extent that he knows algebra at all, knows what he knows precisely; but the seasoned art-critic can never have knowledge more precise than the nature of the subject will allow; and this knowledge can never be as precise as one's knowledge of quadratic equations. It was not different when Valéry became interested in architecture, as he inevitably would; for here was engineering—method—an art with a specific mathematical aspect that could be abstracted from the aesthetic. But his investigation of this subject is cast into a Platonic dialogue, where dialectic permits him to evade direct formulations of the relation of concrete architectural forms to their engineering, or their rationale of method conceived Platonically. Here, even with an art the most mathematical of all after music, he was not able to show that the form was "born" before the "work."

Valéry all his life, as poet, wrote like an Aristotelian; that is, he came to know the "form" (the meaning) in the completed work; but he *talked* like a Platonist whose *ideas* must always precede the *intuition*. I am inclined to believe that he might not have written the prose works (or as many as he did) had his philosophical interests developed after he had written his great poems. The early poems of *Album des Vers Anciens* are the work of a minor symbolist poet who had gone to school to Hérèdia and Mallarmé (with Baudelaire and Poe in the background); these poems could not have revealed to him the deeper movements of his creative powers. Had he not got fixed in the convention of a kind of Platonic Pyrrhonism, the "play" of ideas, which began as youthful intellectual inquiry and continued into old age as the vain mask of the sage, he would have learned from the great poems that the inquiry, *as he conceived it,* into form and intuition was irrelevant to his actual purpose as a poet.

I take it that anybody who has any familiarity at all with "Ebauche d'un Serpent" or "Le Cimetière Marin" would reject the idea that there is form apart from the clusters of symbol which constitute the "intuition"—this, in spite of the somewhat elaborate hocus-pocus which Valéry offers us in his long meditation on the writing of "Le Cimetière Marin." I call it a meditation, though "Fragments de Mémoires d'un Poème," published eighteen years after "Le Cimetière," purports to be an analytical inquiry into the *method* that he had presumably adopted before he began to write the poem. Immensely more resourceful and sophisticated than Poe's "The Philosophy of Composition," "Fragments" is the direct descendant of Poe's essay and perhaps the most distinguished of its hundreds of descendants in what has become a new critical *genre.* This *genre* may be described as the rationalization of the imaginative act, in the attempt to reduce the poem to a pseudo-Cartesian criterion of "clarity" and "distinctness."

The word *method* appears almost obsessively in Valéry's prose: he said many times that after poems were written he felt no interest in *what* he had said in them, but only in *how* he had been able to say it. This quasi-Platonic theory of antecedent form dominates all his writings on poetry, and form he equates with method. In this tradition of critical thought—a tradition which T. S. Eliot has described in his valuable essay, "From Poe to Valéry"—there is the progressive mechanization of the poem and the supremacy of method, until the poem itself becomes an aesthetic machine. The machine produces a calculated effect upon the reader. If this is what Poe and Valéry thought they were doing, they were actually doing something smaller philosophically, and at the same time something poetically greater, than their calculations would have allowed them to do. With Valéry, at any rate, the great poems remain, and his idolatry of method cannot divert our attention from their full and mysterious wholeness. Valéry was a greater poet than his "intellect" wanted him to be; Poe's intellect, narrower than Valéry's, allowed him to see his poems, particularly "The Raven," as greater than he could make them; there is a similar appeal in both from the poetry to omnipotent rationality.

Shortly after Valéry's death T. S. Eliot wrote a short memoir, "Leçon de Valéry," for a volume of *hommages* entitled *Valéry Vivant* (1946); Eliot said:

> He could play different roles, but never lost himself in any. Of some great men, one's prevailing impression may be of goodness, or of inspiration, or of wisdom; I think the prevailing impression one received of Valéry was of intelligence.

Eliot's remarks would justify, I think, the addition of an adjective—an impression of *uncommitted* intelligence. In "L'Idée Fixe" (1932) Valéry had written:

> Je fabrique ma petite terminologie, suivant mes besoins.... Ces sont mes outils intimes. Je me fais mes ustensiles, et les fais pour moi seul: aussi individuels et adoptés que possible a ma maniére de concevoir, et de combiner.

> Vous n'êtes pas denué d'orgueil [says his interlocutor; then Valéry continues:]

> En quoi? Est-ce Robinson vous semble plus orgueilleux que quiconque? Je me considère comme un Robinson intellectuel.

An intellectual Robinson Crusoe improvising his tools and his philosophical food and shelter is a characteristic irony; for Valéry's intellectual pride was so great that he could not accept a philosophy that offered ontological truth. Such "truth," *si arbitraire ou si absurde,* it is only necessary to develop a little *pour rendre cette pensée ridicule, ou odieuse, ou naïve.*

This side of Valéry is so well-known that I may seem to labor it. But since, with his death, a great literary tradition may have come to an end, I wish to explain it to myself a little more precisely than would be desirable were post-symbolism still a powerful force.

I know of no more engaging image of the angelic intellect than that of Robinson Crusoe: an intellect that is self-sufficient, starting from scratch, an intellect not only "unaided" in the theological sense, but dispensing with the great European philosophical traditions and relying upon its own improvisations. The situation of Robinson Crusoe on his island is that of the society without arts, which Plato said must "live by chance," limited in its power to accumulate surpluses of material goods or of spiritual resources. By "arts" the Greeks meant techniques, our technologies. Yet by analogy the intellectual improvisation must likewise rely upon chance, moving from one *petite terminologie* to another—*suivant mes besoins.*

Some ten years after Valéry had been acclaimed in France as the greatest living poet, he published a small book entitled *Littérature,* which I suppose contains more wisdom about the possibilities and limits of poetry than any other work of this century. Between the extremes of the classical and the romantic sensibility the poet of our time, cast up on Crusoe's island, and living by chance, may arrive by a sufficient cunning at an art which occupies the entire stretch between the extremes. I shall quote a long passage from *Littérature* because it seems to me that Valéry is talking about himself, defining what he thought he had done as poet (and perhaps in the greater poems, did):

Since the advent of romanticism *singularity* has been imitated instead of, as in the past, *mastery*.

The instinct of imitation has been the same. But to it the modern has added a contradiction.

Mastery, as the word indicates, is to appear to have command over the technical resources of an art —instead of being visibly commanded by them.

The acquisition of mastery then presupposes the acquired habit of always thinking, or combining, with the technical means as *point of departure*, and of never thinking of a work except in terms of its means.

The contradiction of modernism lies in the end in the impossibility of relating the singular to anything else, of combining it with another singular, since each intuition of the singular, being unique, defies the means: a method of the singular is thus a contradiction in terms. Valéry adds:

But it sometimes happens that mastery is taken off its guard and overcome by some innovator who by *chance* [italics mine], or by gift, creates *new technical means* and seems at first to have given the world a new work. But it is never more than a question of technique.

He is not to be reproached if here, as elsewhere, he fails to solve the ultimate problem of poetry, which is the relation of the means to the subject. We are concerned only with his characteristic way of allowing for innovation or singularity. Since the classical method as starting-point cannot deal with innovation, the innovation of singularity hits upon the right means *by chance*; and he adds, *or by gift*, as a question-begging afterthought.

Singularity as an effect to be aimed at, rather than a quality of the poet's mind which suffuses the work as a secondary quality, is no doubt the hallmark of romanticism. Singularity would thus be the element of chance for the classical sensibility, but for the romantic, the means itself is hit upon by luck. The intolerable burden of the romantic sensibility cannot depend upon an objective continuity of forms and techniques. Yet it is important to remember that Valéry holds that it is only technique which counts in the end.

He seems to have conducted from youth to old age a circular argument in which means and ends chase each other round a ring, but which is the pursuer and which the pursued it is impossible to determine. Technique, or mastery of the means, would appear to be the only possible object of calculation, the focus of "clear and distinct ideas"; and I suspect that Valéry's dialectic was doomed to irresolution by his Cartesian dualism, which made a clean break between sensibility and "ideas." But in glancing at the great poems, we shall not be able to believe of Valéry, any more than of Poe, that his techniques were as calculated as he thought, or tried to think, or tried to make us think.

If we eliminated from Valéry's poems five titles there would be little left to justify his great reputation: he would be a minor post-Symbolist poet of the school of Mallarmé. I suppose it is generally agreed that the principal poems are "La Jeune Parque," "La Pythie," "Fragments du 'Narcisse,' " "L'Ébauche d'un Serpent," and "Le Cimetière Marin." Since my first acquaintance with these poems I have had difficulty with them, for I can never be sure that I have got them in my ear. (Mr. Justin O'Brien, Mr. Wallace Fowlie, and Mr. Jackson Mathews are perhaps the only American French scholars who can possess the auditory meaning of French verse.) The late Yvor Winters believed that "L'Ébauche d'un Serpent" is the greatest poem in any language. I wonder how he could be sure; but I am sure that it is a very great poem, though I prefer "Le Cimetière Marin" (which Winters acknowledged to be great); and in trying to set forth a few of the reasons why

I think this I shall say all that I know enough to say about
the poetics of Paul Valéry.

There is something a little haphazard about Valéry's development as a poet, in the sense that from the early nineties to
his death in 1945 there is no clear line of development of
either subject or methods—in spite of his obsessive preoccupation with method. There seems to have been a sudden burst
of imaginative energy which lasted about five years, during
which he wrote the "great" poems; and he then subsided.
From this, it does not necessarily follow, as Winters seemed
to think, that Valéry must therefore be a lesser poet than
Baudelaire, though for other reasons I think he probably is.
Baudelaire produced one book, and he very early set out to
do so. But apart from the structure of *Les Fleurs du Mal* as a
single work, we could extract eight or ten poems which for
range and depth of experience and of consciousness might
surpass any similar selection from Valéry. Yet it would be difficult to find any *single poem* by Baudelaire that comes as near
perfection in intellectual structure, and in implicit imagery,
as the two great Valéry poems. By implicit imagery I mean a
kind of unity of idea and symbol, so that most markedly in
the "Cimetière" one never knows whether the "argument" is
really there, or exists only in our sense of it. The development
of the "Serpent" is somewhat different: the argument is
formidable and paraphraseable. I shall comment on this, and
in the course of doing so comment on Winters' brilliant commentary.

Winters' statement of the theme of the poem is elaborate
and, I think, exact, and it seems to me to exhaust the rational
content. But there is a good deal of the poem left over, after
the paraphrase; and it is this residue which seems to me intractable and even obscure beyond any obscurity that one may
find even in "La Jeune Parque," a poem which Albert
Thibaudet called the most obscure in French literature. I
shall not quote Winters, but shall refer the interested reader
to his analysis in the essay "Problems for the Modern Critic

of Literature." Winters sums up his statement of the theme as follows: "The theme is the most inclusive of tragic themes: one might describe it as the theme of tragedy."

I am inclined to doubt that this is true, in the sense that I doubt that tragedy ever quite exhibits a *theme* as such apart from tragic *action*. What Winters describes as the theme of tragedy seems to me to be merely the historic paradox of imperfection and evil existing in a world that we can imagine only if we assume that it was created by a perfect being. God compromising and limiting his perfection, in the act of creating the material universe, is the theme of the "Serpent"; it is an ancient theme which received its philosophical formulation by the disciples of Plotinus—Iamblichus and Porphyry—and earlier informed the various Gnostic accounts of the mystery of evil. It is a great theme, and it allowed Valéry to write a great poem. But I believe that the magnificent residue of image, the subtle interplay of thought and sub-rational perception between Eve and the Serpent, is involved in an argument which we must scrutinize on its own merits, like any other philosophical position. And this argument seems to me deeply disappointing in a man of Valéry's supposed philosophical resources. In stanza sixteen, the Serpent, addressing Eve, says:

> O chair mollement décidée,
> Sans que je t'eusse intimidée,
> A chanceler dans la splendeur!
> Bientôt, je t'aurai, je parie,
> Déjà ta nuance varie!

The last line here is an excellent example of Valéry's power of reducing his argument to a sensuous image, and the triumph of the poem largely consists in the poet's immense invention in this linguistic virtuosity which the French language far more than English allows.

What Winters called the tragic theme proceeds from the Gnostic theory of evil. The despair of the Serpent is his Gnosis of this evil, for it is knowledge of evil alone which constitutes evil for created beings. Hence the Serpent's despair; and hence the fact that he has only despair to offer to God. Sin seems to be a little shadowy in this scene, in spite of the magnificent imagery in which Valéry presents the Serpent's temptation of Eve. Winters points out the absence of Adam: he is not necessary to this intellectual drama, since it is not action but knowledge which dooms the Serpent, who is a surrogate of Adam. Winters' commentary is not only of great value in itself; it compels one to reconsider the structure of the poem. Valéry's version of the myth seems to me a little off-center, a little "rigged," although marvelously inventive. May we ask what he might have done with the full, traditional body of the myth? We shall not at any rate get an answer. I hope that I am not invading the privacy of Paul Valéry's mind when I suggest that the Serpent is a methodologist too: that he is not interested in Eve (as Adam presumably was), that he is concerned with the method, not the action or the consequence, of temptation, and that the Gnostic philosophy of the Serpent is the inevitable projection of a mind obsessed with method.

I shall bring these observations to a close with a few cursory remarks on the "Cimetière." This poem has been inundated with analysis, beginning with Valéry's own. It seems to me a much greater poem than the "Serpent," and its greatness was made possible because its subject did not contain the temptations to philosophical eccentricities that Valéry's private myth of Eden offered. The "Cimetière" has no myth. It is a meditation in the poet's own person upon a symbol which is first of all a natural phenomenon—the sea: the symbol is grounded in one of the eternal phenomenal mysteries. It has been suggested to me that the meaning of the title is: The Sea as Graveyard. We are not given a "philosophy" which we are tempted to argue with: the philosophy of "Le Cimetière Marin" is not reducible. If there is greater poetry in French or English in this century than the last stanza, I have not seen it:

Le vent se lève! ... il faut tenter de vivre!
L'air immense ouvre et referme mon livre,
La vague en poudre ose jaillir des rocs!
Envolez-vous, pages tout éblouies!
Rompez, vagues! Rompez d'eaux réjouies
Ce toit tranquille où picoraient des focs!

Shadow

A Parable and a Polemic

1963

TO SAY THAT form is a problem is to say two things: that it is a problem that may some day be solved. What else is a problem for? Our metaphor here has always contained a hidden analogy to mathematics, perhaps a sort of equation: form equals content, or content equals form. This equation may mean something in the abstract discussion of poetry and other arts, but I dare say it is not very useful for active literary criticism. Or the form-content equation could conceal another kind of metaphor—the container and the thing contained. But which is the container and which the contained? Here we introduce—or for centuries have introduced—a spatial notion: something is *in* something else. There have always been people who hold that *this* something wanted to be in *that* something, and is happy to be there. These people we call formalists. Other people have held that the first something never wanted to be in the second, and if it *is* in, it must get out; furthermore, the time comes round when it will not try to get in, but will be henceforth and forever free. These amiable, if somewhat restless, people we may call any number of things; at the moment I shall designate them expressionists.

It must be obvious to persons who have read a little poetry, off and on, most of their lives, that poets (not the abstract poet) are always partly formalist, partly expressionist; but at certain times they are a little more of the one than of the other, or even a great deal more. The expressionists rely upon a quite respectable metaphor which lurks in the Latin verb: *exprimere,* which I remind myself means to press or squeeze out. The reason why expressionists may be called different names is that it is possible to imagine so many things being squeezed out of so many other things. The first expressionist was no doubt the god who squeezed the wind out of a bag and left it up to Odysseus to get it back in; but he too, or his agent, Odysseus, must have been partly a formalist or he could not have recovered the wind, in order to squeeze it out again. (We all know that the wind has blown more than once.)

The particular bias of my own view of this matter I had better at this point make clear: it is hard for me to think of anything being squeezed that does not eventually (I'm aware of the pun) emit wind. If we cling to the squeezing figure with some of the consistency with which John Donne is said to have clung to his figures, we may perform the act of transference which Aristotle called, in Greek, metaphor, and see as a species of wind the paint that an artist may squeeze out of a tube. I believe that both Aristotle and Donne would allow a further transference. Our language will not permit us to say: The hurricane brought an eighty-mile *breath;* but the Greeks could say it; for the howl of wind was the howl of breath, *pneuma* being the single word for both. The further extension that I was asking Aristotle's permission to make is howling paint; other extensions might be howling sculpture and howling architecture, but more particularly howling music, music being nearer to the vehicle of the metaphor because it is sound. Have I failed to point out that there is also howling poetry? I forbear to elucidate the steps by which we have arrived at these further extensions.

> The Pow'rs gave Ear, and granted half his Pray'r,
> The rest, the Winds dispersed in empty Air.

The Baron was trying to be a formalist, but the wind knew better; he was half expressionist.

If Pope's Baron was unwittingly an expressionist, Pope himself was not, for he understood his Baron better than the Baron understood himself. Had the Baron been a complete formalist, what would he have done? He would have assayed the complete seduction of Belinda—perhaps sacramentally, all these characters in their prototypes having been good Catholics —but at any rate he would have tried to get, under whatever religious dispensation, or none at all, the complete woman, not a mere lock of hair. It is perhaps a little shocking (it shocks me a little) to suggest that a formalist ought to behave this way. Are not formalists supposed to behave correctly; that is, to do practically nothing? But it is the Baron himself who, as non-formalist, does practically nothing. Instead of an act of adultery, he performs an act of synecdoche, or the act that seeks a part instead of the whole; and this, except in the metonymic world of satire, is the expressionist act. Pope clearly understood that the expressionist is by nature a comic character; the trouble begins only when he begins to take himself seriously. I have said that the Baron does practically nothing; yet he does try to do *something*. Is it not better for the comic expressionist to try to do something than to do nothing but to prophesy to the wind? I believe there is no term in rhetoric for the non-act of preferring nothing to the whole, or nothing to even a small part, like a lock of hair. I take it that in the scale of critical, as well as of moral, values it is better to prefer a lock of hair to the sound of one's own voice.

The argument for expressionism is, of course, that it is interesting and new, interesting perhaps because it is new; and what is new is relevant to our time. The sound of one's own voice is always new because it is the sound of one's own voice; and it is always relevant because its disorder can always be confirmed by the disorder *over yonder*. The idea of relevance is doubtless one of our more obscure safeguards for the perpetuation of disorder, both interior and exterior; for to say that disorderly art is relevant to our time is to assume that we know what our time is. This is one of the more sinister versions of Yvor Winters' fallacy of imitative form. Does not imitative form—the phrase itself must be an oxymoron—does not imitative form mean no form? Does it not mean merely whatever comes up from the bottom?

> A constant *Vapour* o'er the Palace flies
> Strange Phantoms rising as the Mists arise. . . .

These phantoms, from the Cave of Spleen, move into action, directly after the Baron commits his expressionist synecdoche. Ariel, Belinda's guardian, withdraws; the gnome Umbriel, from the Cave of Spleen, takes command. Who is Umbriel? Alas, he is the late Dr. C. G. Jung's Shadow Self which comes up from the bottom and refuses to be assimilated to Ariel, his ego-consciousness, thus rendering him impotent. As a result, the splenetic goddess releases her "vapours" through two engaging allegorical ladies; first, Ill-Nature, and, second, "Affectation with a sickly mien." I believe I am not betraying Pope by reading *neurosis* for *affectation*. Were we not told recently by A. Alvarez that the only poetry relevant to our time is the poetry of the nervous breakdown and of the public confession, the synecdochic sound of one's own voice; in short, howling poetry?

Faulkner's *Sanctuary* and the
Southern Myth
1968

UNTIL I was asked to write this introduction, I had not read *Sanctuary* since shortly after it was first published in 1931. I happened to read it, quite accidentally, in Paris in the early fall of 1932 in the English edition (Chatto & Windus) which John Peale Bishop gave me one day on the terrace of a café in the rue Royale. Hemingway had given it to Bishop, dismissing it as blown-up and no good. I suppose he thought that Bishop, being a Southerner, might understand it better and see good in it. After thirty-six years I can't remember whether Bishop urged me to read *Sanctuary;* simply that he gave it to me. I remember that we talked about another book by Faulkner which had been published a couple of years before *Sanctuary,* and which we had both read. This was *The Sound and the Fury.* We agreed, rather solemnly, as young men habitually do, that it was a work of genius, but imperfect, and derivative of Joyce and Flaubert. I did not then understand the vanity that makes young men enjoy detecting literary influences; so I thought that Joyce in the Benjy section and Flaubert in the Jason section were not assimilated. Here was mere imitation. In 1926 I had put

---

Introduction to the New American Library edition of *Sanctuary.*

Hemingway in his place by suggesting that his style was a mixture of Captain Marryat and Defoe: it *was* that, but it was also a great deal more than an imitation of any eighteenth-century English author. A few days after John Bishop gave me that copy of *Sanctuary* I read it through at a sitting.

In the three years between 1929 and 1932 William Faulkner had published three novels which in my opinion are his masterpieces: *The Sound and the Fury, As I Lay Dying,* and *Light in August.* Other critics might argue for *Absalom, Absalom!, The Wild Palms,* or *The Hamlet*; but nobody would omit from a list of Faulkner's best novels *The Sound and the Fury.* And no critic has included, in a list of the best, *Sanctuary*; but I do include it, although one would have to place it near the bottom. It is well above *A Fable,* which seems to me a mediocre calamity. No matter: there is no common law of literature which compels a writer to get better and better, year after year. And it is not important that *A Fable, The Town,* and *The Reivers* show little of Faulkner's genius.

With Faulkner in mind, I should like to suggest an historical moment for the climax of what has been called the Southern Renaissance. I would put it near the middle nineteen-thirties, at the high point of William Faulkner's creative period. I cannot believe that American readers make the mistake of a brilliant French critic, Michel Mohrt, who about ten years ago wrote a book on the *American* novel from which an unalert reader might get the impression that the *Southern* novel consists entirely of William Faulkner, Robert Penn Warren, and Truman Capote. Certainly Faulkner and Warren are a large part of it; but they are not all of it. If literary history has no laws, it nevertheless shows us empirically that a writer of Faulkner's magnitude has seldom appeared alone, in complete social isolation—though, like Faulkner and Hawthorne, he may isolate himself personally in order to avoid literary cliques and to concentrate on his work.

Before I try to "place" *Sanctuary* it may be useful to say something about the situation of the South from 1865 to about

1918 or the early 1920s. It must be borne in mind that neither
Faulkner nor any other Southern writer had a fully developed,
self-conscious historical sense. A novelist's historical sense is
usually merely implicit in his immediate response to his material—in Faulkner's case, Yoknapatawpha County. The Southern situation, as we may see it in retrospect, will throw some
light upon Faulkner and his great part in the so-called Southern Renaissance. Or should we call it the Southern Naissance?
For the antebellum South produced only Poe, Simms, Timrod,
and Cable, and the period between the Civil War and World
War I only the apprentice works of James Branch Cabell and
Ellen Glasgow; in neither period were there enough writers of
the first order to constitute a literature. The political secession
of the South occurred in 1861, the moral secession after 1865,
and this lasted until the end of World War I.

Isolation by the kind of choice that results from defeat and
poverty made the Southern states virtually a separate nation,
or at least a colonial province ruled until 1877 by the con-
querors, and exploited by their heirs until yesterday: the
South was Uncle Sam's Other Province. This social situation
produced a sentimental literature of Narcissism, in which the
South tried to define itself by looking into a glass behind its
back: not inward. It was thus not a literature of introspection,
but a literature of romantic illusion; and its mode was what I
have called elsewhere the Rhetorical Mode. I like Yeats' epi-
gram about rhetoric—it is the way we quarrel with others, not
ourselves—and rhetoric in the Reconstruction South was a
good way of quarreling with the Yankees, who were to blame
for everything. The quarrel raged with some cunning and
versatility, for it elicited a good deal of fiction in which the
Southern gentleman was the Chevalier Bayard *redivivus*, the
Poor White a picturesque buffoon who spoke a quaint dialect,
and the Negro Rousseau's Natural Man spoiled by having
been deprived of the benefits of slavery.

Two exceptions must be noticed, for they made all the difference, or were eventually to do so. The first appeared in the

antebellum South: Augustus Baldwin Longstreet's *Georgia Scenes*, a series of yarns and anecdotes of the life of the Crackers and Red Necks of the Low Country. These are comic characters, but they are observed with precision, and they are presented as complete, serious human beings, not as stereotypes, or even types. But *Georgia Scenes*, published in 1835, is not "folk literature"; it was written over a number of years by an educated man, a judge and a college president, for the delectation (a word that Longstreet might have used) of his peers. The second crucial work was published forty-five years later, just after the Reconstruction. This was Mark Twain's *Huckleberry Finn*, the first Southern novel in which the action is generated inside the characters. It is not, perhaps, the masterpiece that the academic Mark Twain "industry" has made it out to be; yet for the reason I have indicated, it is a work of great originality and historical importance. These two works are the beginning of modern Southern literature; they are also important for American literature as a whole. What concerns me here is the lessons they taught a great novelist of the twentieth century: the one a lesson in the necessity of direct observation of character and scene; the other the indispensable lesson that the art of fiction begins with inner conflict, not in a quarrel with a wicked enemy to the North, or anywhere else. William Faulkner was a master, the greatest of our time, of authentic observation and of the inner conflict.

Yet these lessons might not have been learned, even by Faulkner, but for two historical forces that seemed to converge dramatically at the end of World War I. The Reconstruction of the South was completed, and even accepted by the South, on the condition that the race problem be left in Southern hands. For the South was becoming industrialized and thus an enthusiastic participant in the benefits of the Union—in short, getting rich again. Some recusants remained, chiefly young men disaffected by the war experience of 1917-18 and bemused by the violent transition from the Old South to the irresistible new. They had been in Europe, where the literary young men

—Davidson, Ransom, Bishop, Faulkner, many others—had
become aware of the great European writers of the half-
century preceding them: Baudelaire, Rimbaud, Proust, and
now Joyce; and for the first time (so far as I know) Henry
James was read by Southerners as an artist, not merely as a
novelist of manners. The re-entry of the South into the world
and the violent social changes at home brought about a new
consciousness which was able to learn the lessons of Longstreet and Mark Twain and to apply them to a vastly larger
historical sense. This consciousness generated an image of the
past in the present. And this image is the pervasive Southern
subject of our time. Faulkner did not have to learn it. He was
born with it and grew up with it, and he was perfectly conscious of it when he made Gavin Stevens say, in *Requiem for
a Nun*: "The past is not dead. It is not even the past."

I have had to simplify. Perhaps I have made too schematic
a complex historical situation; and I have doubtless so exag-
gerated the value of Longstreet and Twain as to place them
as "influences" that were consciously assimilated by a generation of Southern writers. I had better back off a little and call
them forerunners. Yet Mark Twain and Longstreet give us the
Southern frontier—Twain the frontier of the Old Southwest,
Longstreet the frontier of the southeastern seaboard. The
Southern frontier was not a locality, but an economy and a
social structure; a culture, in fact, which has lasted into our
time and which we can observe in the Snopeses and the Varners, frontier types corrupted by access to the money economy
of the plantation system.

What Faulkner learned from his forerunners—and Warren
and Andrew Lytle a decade later—might be described as a
technique of observation, a way of seeing the Southern rural
types, both white and Negro, not as picturesque eccentrics in
a setting of local color, but as characters in depth, complex
and, like all other people, ultimately mysterious. But we shall
not be able to estimate the larger literary influences that
Faulkner felt until he has been dead at least twenty years. At

present they seem to have been Twain, Longstreet, Dickens, Flaubert, and Joyce. What Faulkner evidently learned from Flaubert was a technique of cutting off a group of characters from himself and relating them to one another in an enclosed scene, such as we find in the opening chapters of *Sanctuary* leading up to the corncob rape of Temple Drake at the Old Frenchman Place. The lesson of Joyce is more easily discerned: it is everywhere in Faulkner, not as imitation but as a method so adapted to his purposes as to be a vehicle of his own originality. One may cite only the Benjy section of *The Sound and the Fury*, where the level of Benjy's perception is the inchoate "stream of consciousness" of an idiot; yet the exposition objectifies the blur of Benjy's mind by means of formal grammatical predication. This is a brilliant adaptation of Joyce.

Whether my guess as to the causes of the literary awakening of the South at the end of the first world war is true or not, there was, however one explains it, frenetic literary activity after 1918 that has scarcely abated yet. In the twenties and early thirties most of the Southern writers whose reputations we now take for granted appeared in the Southern "little magazines." I am not concerned here with the poets; so I shall merely allude to *The Fugitive*, in Nashville, where Ransom, Davidson, and Warren were first published. *The Double Dealer* in New Orleans published Faulkner's first work— poems and reviews. The index of *The Southern Review*, published in Baton Rouge from 1935 to 1942, would be a roll call of the best Southern writers of this century: Katherine Anne Porter, Caroline Gordon, Andrew Lytle, Robert Penn Warren, Eudora Welty, Carson McCullers, Stark Young, Elizabeth Madox Roberts.

These are the leading fiction writers of the older generation, with Faulkner at the head of the table; and they are sufficient evidence that he did not rise out of a cultural vacuum. Other critics have perceived what they consider the anomaly of Mississippi. How could the most "backward" state in the Union produce not only William Faulkner but Stark Young, Roark Bradford, and Eudora Welty—all very different from one another but all *very* Mississippi? Yeats gave the best answer to this question when he was asked how Ireland could have had a literary renaissance in the first decade of this century. He said, in effect, that poverty and ignorance had made it possible. There is no real paradox in giving Yeats' answer to the same question about Mississippi after 1918. Poverty, and the ignorance that attends poverty, had isolated the common people—the Snopeses, the Varners, the Bundrens—with the result that their language retained an *illiterate* purity, uncorrupted by the "correct" English of half-educated schoolteachers, or by sociological jargon, or by the conditioned reflex language of advertising; while at the same time a small minority in Mississippi (and in other Southern states) maintained at a high level of sophistication a *literate* purity of diction based upon the old traditions of classical humanism. The majority could not read at all; a small minority could not only read but could read Latin and cap verses from Horace and Vergil. This was scarcely a democratic situation, but I daresay one must take one's literature where one finds it, under whatever social conditions will allow it to flourish.

The first-rate Southern poets of the twenties and thirties were few: Ransom, Warren, Davidson, and—as a poet she is unknown today—Elizabeth Madox Roberts. The preoccupation with the obsessive Southern subject, the past in the present, is obviously a social and historical interest, best approached through the form that Henry James elevated to the rank of true history. If the Southern Renaissance has not been a flash in the pan, it will continue in the Southern novel.

What, then, has been the imaginative focus of the Southern novel of our time? Malcolm Cowley once described it as "William Faulkner's Legend of the South," supposing no doubt that Faulkner had invented it. And Faulkner, in a letter to Cowley while Cowley was getting together the *Portable Faulkner*, said that he was not conscious of a legend. That was as it should be if the legend was to be imaginatively effective. For it was more than a legend, it was a myth; and it was every Southerner's myth from 1865 to about 1940, or up to World War II. Had Faulkner invented the myth, it would not have been as good as it was for his purposes; nor would the myth of Oedipus, had Sophocles invented it. For the Southern legend is a true myth which informed the sensibility and thought, at varying conscious levels, of the defeated South. (By myth I mean a dramatic projection of heroic action, or of the tragic failure of heroic action, upon the reality of the common life of a society, so that the myth *is* reality.)

The outlines of the Southern myth shift and vary with one's degree of self-consciousness. I see it somewhat as follows: the South, afflicted with the curse of slavery—a curse, like that of Original Sin, for which no single person is responsible—had to be destroyed, the good along with the evil. The old order had a great deal of good, one of the "goods" being a result of the evil; for slavery itself entailed a certain moral responsibility which the capitalist employer in free societies did not need to exercise if it was not his will to do so. This old order, in which the good could not be salvaged from the bad, was replaced by a new order which was in many ways worse than the old. The Negro, legally free, was not prepared for freedom; nobody was trying to prepare him. The carpetbaggers, "foreign" exploiters, and their collaborators, the native rascals called "scalawags," gave the Old South its final agonies. The cynical materialism of the new order brought to the South the American standard of living, but it also brought about a society similar to that which Matthew Arnold saw in the North in the eighties and called vigorous and uninteresting.

The evil of slavery was twofold, for the "peculiar institution" not only used human beings for a purpose for which God had not intended them; it made it possible for the white man to misuse and exploit nature herself for his own power and glory. The exploitation of nature is a theme that runs through all Faulkner's work; it adds a philosophical, even a mystical, dimension to the conventional Southern myth. For most of us the myth is merely historical and secular. It is not, as I look back to the time when it could be taken for granted, a myth of the cosmic Greek order in which the gods took part. But it did very well for the novel, as well perhaps as the New England myth of *The House of the Seven Gables*, which the Southern myth somewhat resembles. Yet the differences are important. The classical theocratic culture of New England merely declined; its decline could not be focused upon a great action in which the entire society was involved. But the Southern culture did not decline (so the myth goes); it was destroyed by outsiders in a Trojan war. The "older" culture of Troy-South was wiped out by the "upstart" culture of Greece-North. *Sunt lacrimae rerum;* and the Yankees were therefore to blame for everything—until, as I have pointed out, the time of World War I.

This myth, inadequate as it may appear to the non-Southern reader, has permitted a generation of Southern novelists to understand and to dramatize (that is, to depict in action) much of the Southern historical reality. In Faulkner, the outlines of the myth vary from novel to novel. Perhaps he developed it most fully in *Absalom, Absalom!* and *The Sound and the Fury*. This is not the place to go through the novels and to try to see what the myth does with—or does to—the great cast of characters that Faulkner created. Just one example: may we not discern in Quentin Compson's flight to Harvard the flight of Aeneas from Troy, and may we not imagine the shadow of Quentin's weak father clinging, like Anchises, to his son's back? Here the myth breaks off; for Quentin had no Rome to found and, crushed by the weight of the past, he committed suicide.

The mythical outlines of *Sanctuary* are plain enough, but one must not expect the myth to be developed in an heroic action. The action is anti-heroic; or perhaps one might say more precisely that in spite of the violence of the rape of

Temple and the lynching of Lee Goodwin, there is no action at all. Horace Benbow, a scion of the Old South, is morally impotent; he ought to be able to save Lee Goodwin from the false charge of the murder of old Tommy, who would have been a legal witness to the rape of Temple Drake by Popeye. Temple's father, Judge Drake, in order to conceal her sojourn in a Memphis brothel, indirectly allies himself with Popeye, and allows Goodwin to be convicted. Judge Drake, in short, is the Old South corrupted, as Benbow is the Old South morally bankrupt. Temple herself is Southern womanhood: passive, destructive, and without the sense of right and wrong. I hesitate to describe her as amoral; amoral is a hybrid word. She is what psychiatrists call a psychopathic personality, dominated by compulsions and lacking in real emotions. Clarence Snopes appears as blackmailer and *agent provocateur*. The weak Gowan Stevens, Temple's "date," gets drunk and abandons her, and Southern womanhood cannot protect itself. All the upper-class characters, except Benbow, move from weakness to corruption. Temple's perjury in the courtroom seals Goodwin's fate, and Popeye goes free. Benbow remains pure but defeated. We last see Temple with her father in the Luxembourg Gardens. He has taken her to France to sit out the scandal. In the final chapter there is an awkward shift to Popeye's boyhood, and we are told that he came to his end in Alabama by being hanged for the murder of a policeman.

Awkward as the conclusion may be, and anti-climatic as the mere expository account of Popeye and Temple is at the end, it is difficult to imagine a resolution to the violence at the center of the novel. There is nothing to be resolved. The action consists of a series of incidents, some of them, like the gangster's funeral and the country boys at Miss Reba's brothel, having little relation to the central situation: a series of incidents in which the action is non-action, for violence is not action but merely activity. Critics have called *Sanctuary* a *tour de force*, in the sense of "shocker." It *is* shocking; but the *tour de force* I believe has a more serious significance. To sustain one's interest in a novel of some three hundred pages in which there are characters but no action is a triumph of virtuosity.

Three Commentaries
Poe, James, and Joyce
1950

I. The Fall of the House of Usher

THIS FAMOUS story is perhaps not Poe's best, but it has significant features which ought to illuminate some of the later, more mature work in the naturalistic-symbolic technique of Flaubert, Joyce, and James. Poe's insistence upon unity of effect, from first word to last, in the famous review of Hawthorne's *Twice-Told Tales*, anticipates from one point of view the high claims of James in his essay "The Art of Fiction." James asserts that the imaginative writer must take his art at least as seriously as the historian takes his; that is to say, he must no longer apologize, he must not say "it *may* have happened this way"; he must, since he cannot rely upon the reader's acceptance of known historical incident, create the illusion of reality, so that the reader may have a "direct impression" of it. It was toward this complete achievement of "direct impression" that Poe was moving, in his tales and in his criticism; he, like Hawthorne, was a great forerunner. The reasons why he did not himself fully achieve it (perhaps less even than Hawthorne) are perceptible in "The Fall of the House of Usher."

Like Hawthorne again, Poe seems to have been very little

influenced by the common-sense realism of the eighteenth-century English novel. What has been known in our time as the romantic sensibility reached him from two directions: the Gothic tale of Walpole and Monk Lewis, and the poetry of Coleridge. Roderick Usher is a "Gothic" character taken seriously; that is to say, Poe takes the Gothic setting, with all its machinery and *décor*, and the preposterous Gothic hero, and transforms them into the material of serious literary art. Usher becomes the prototype of the Joycean and Jamesian hero who cannot function in the ordinary world. He has two characteristic traits of this later fictional hero of our own time. First, he is afflicted with the split personality of the manic depressive:

> His action was alternately vivacious and sullen. His voice varied rapidly from a tremulous indecision (when the animal spirits seemed utterly in abeyance) to that species of energetic concision... and perfectly modulated guttural utterance, which may be observed in the lost drunkard, or the irreclaimable eater of opium, during the periods of his most intense excitement.

Secondly, certain musical sounds (for some unmusical reason Poe selects the notes of the guitar) are alone tolerable to him: "He suffered from a morbid acuteness of the sense." He cannot live in the real world; he is constantly exacerbated. At the same time he "has a passionate devotion to the intricacies... of musical science"; and his paintings are "pure abstractions" which have "an intensity of intolerable awe."

Usher is, of course, both our old and our new friend; his new name is Monsieur Teste, and much of the history of modern French literature is in that name. Usher's "want of moral energy," along with a hypertrophy of sensibility and intellect in a split personality, places him in the ancestry of Gabriel Conroy, Stephen Daedalus, John Marcher, J. Alfred Prufrock,

Mrs. Dalloway—a forbear of whose somewhat showy acces-
sories they might well be a little ashamed; or they might enjoy
a degree of moral complacency in contemplating their own
luck in having had greater literary artists than Poe present
them to us in a more credible imaginative reality.

I have referred to the Gothic trappings and the poetry of
Coleridge as the sources of Poe's romanticism. In trying to
understand the kind of unity of effect that Poe demanded of
the writer of fiction we must bear in mind two things. First,
unity of *plot*, the emphasis upon which led him to the invention of the "tale of ratiocination." But plot is not so necessary
to the serious story of moral perversion of which "The Fall of
the House of Usher," "Ligeia," and "Morella" are Poe's supreme examples. Secondly, the unity of tone, a quality that
had not been consciously aimed at in fiction before Poe. It is
this particular kind of unity, a poetical rather than a fictional
characteristic, which Poe must have got from the Romantic
poets, Coleridge especially, and from Coleridge's criticism as
well as "Kubla Khan" and "Christabel." Unity of plot and
tone can exist without the *created, active detail* which came
into this tradition of fiction with Flaubert, to be perfected
later by James, Chekhov, and Joyce.

In "The Fall of the House of Usher," *there is not one instance of dramatized detail.* Although Poe's first-person narrator is in direct contact with the scene, he merely reports it;
he does not show us scene and character in action; it is all
description. The closest approach in the entire story to active
detail is the glimpse, at the beginning, that the narrator gives
us of the furtive doctor as he passes him on "one of the stair-
cases." If we contrast the remoteness of Poe's reporting in the
entire range of this story with the brilliant re-creation of the
character of Michael Furey by Gretta Conroy in "The Dead,"
we shall be able to form some conception of the advance in the
techniques of reality that was achieved in the sixty-odd years
between Poe and Joyce. The powerful description of the fa-
çade of the House of Usher, as the narrator approaches it, sets

up unity of tone, but the description is never woven into the action of the story: the "metaphysical" identity of scene and character reaches our consciousness through *lyrical assertion*. The fissure in the wall of the house remains an inert symbol of Usher's split personality. At the climax of the story Poe uses an incredibly clumsy device in the effort to make the collapse of Usher active dramatically; that is, he employs the mechanical device of coincidence. The narrator is reading to Usher the absurd tale of the "Mad Trist" of Sir Lancelot Canning. The knight has slain the dragon and now approaches the "brazen shield," which falls with tremendous clatter. Usher has been "hearing" it, but what he has been actually hearing is the rending of the lid of his sister Madeline's coffin and the grating of the iron door of the tomb; until at the end the sister (who has been in a cataleptic trance) stands outside Usher's door. The door opens; she stands before them. The narrator flees and the House of Usher, collapsing, sinks forever with its master into the waters of the "tarn."

We could dwell upon the symbolism of the identity of house and master, of the burial alive of Madeline, of the fissure in the wall of the house and the fissure in the psyche of Usher. What we should emphasize here is the dominance of symbolism over its visible base: symbolism external and "lyrical," not intrinsic and dramatic. The active structure of the story is mechanical and thus negligible; but its lyrical structure is impressive. Poe's plots seem most successful when the reality of scene and character is of secondary importance in the total effect; that is, in the tale of "ratiocination." He seemed unable to combine incident with his gift for "insight symbolism"; as a result his symbolic tales are insecurely based upon scenic reality. But the insight was great. In Roderick Usher, as we have said, we get for the first time the hero of modern fiction. In the history of literature the discoverer of the subject is almost never the perfector of the techniques for making the subject real.

II. The Beast in the Jungle

James' "The Beast in the Jungle" was first published in 1903 in a volume of short stories entitled *The Better Sort*. It was written at about the same time as Joyce's "The Dead," and although the fables of the two stories differ as profoundly as their techniques, they invite comparison at several levels. Both stories hinge upon climaxes of self-revelation, and both limit the reader's access to the subject to a central intelligence; both end with a powerful irony which we may call "classical irony" because its appearance has been predicted by the reader, whose interest is thus engaged at a higher level than that of mere surprise. We know that John Marcher and Gabriel Conroy are failing in some fundamental insight into their predicaments: our suspense looks ahead to the revelation of this failure to themselves. It comes, in both stories, in a short-view scene, toward which our interest has been directed in mounting intensity.

Again, as in "The Fall of the House of Usher" and "The Dead," we have the embodiment of the great contemporary subject: the isolation and the frustration of personality. It is a subject that goes back also to Poe's "William Wilson" and to Hawthorne in "The Bosom Serpent" and "Young Goodman Brown." Poe's method is nearer than Hawthorne's to the modern technique which grounds in psychological realism the symbolic representation of the hero's egoism. Hawthorne tends to scant the realistic base and to let his symbols become attenuated into allegory. But it is a fact of curious and perhaps of important historical interest that Hawthorne was the first American writer (he may have anticipated everyone in Europe) who was conscious of the failure of modern man to realize his full capacity for moral growth. In four entries in the *American Notebooks* he plays with this problem as the theme of a possible story, and he actually states the theme of "The Beast in the Jungle" some sixty years before the story was written:

> A young man and a girl meet together, each in search
> of a person to be known by some peculiar sign. They
> watch and wait a great while for that person to pass.
> At last special circumstance discloses that each is the
> one that the other is waiting for. Moral—that what
> we need for our happiness is often close at hand, if
> we knew but how to seek it.

To distinguish certain features of the method of "The Beast
in the Jungle" we could scarcely do better than to use some of
James' own critical terms. The "story," reduced to the slight
action through which James develops the values of the situation, can be told very briefly. At a party John Marcher meets
May Bartram; they renew a casual acquaintance of ten years
before. Miss Bartram reminds him of a remarkable confession
that he had made on that occasion: he had seen himself as a
man to whom something overwhelming was destined to happen, and his part in life, excluding all other aims, was to await
it—something special, even unique, for which he was to hold
himself in readiness. He still feels the imminence of his des-
tiny: it may come at any moment. Marcher and Miss Bartram
now enter into a long, uncommitted relationship from which
she gets nothing and he all that he can allow himself to get,
since he must accept nothing short of his supreme moment.
What he gets in the long run is her life, but he cannot "use" it
since he can give nothing in return. They drift, in this moral
stalemate, into middle age. Miss Bartram dies. Marcher feels
increasingly empty and abandoned, and forms the habit of
haunting her grave (one thinks here of the related story "The
Altar of the Dead"), until one day he looks into the eyes of
another man haunting another grave. The man's eyes expose
the depths of grief. The revelation forces Marcher into a tragic
and ironic awareness. The supreme value for which he had
reserved his life he had, of course, killed: it lay in the grave of
May Bartram.

The story is laid out in six sections, and the point of view is consistently that of Marcher. The two first sections constitute a long foreground or "complication." It may be questioned whether the long complication is justified, since in it nothing "happens": in only about twice the space James lays the foreground of a very long novel, *The Ambassadors*. There are only two short-view scenes in the story. In slighting the scenic effect it is possible that James has violated one of his primary canons: the importance of rendition over statement. (There is too much of the elaborate voice of James, what Mr. Edmund Wilson has harshly described as the "Jamesian gas.") Yet one can see that he could not allow himself to get too deeply into Marcher's consciousness, at the stage of the complication, or Marcher himself would have had to examine his illusion too closely, and the story would have collapsed. The reader may well wonder whether the two brief scenic moments, when they finally come, are adequately prepared for, in spite of the length of preparation. James has not, in the first three sections, made either Marcher or Miss Bartram a *visible* character; he has merely presented their enveloping fate, as it *could* have been seen from Marcher's point of view; but we have seen them not quite credibly.

The excessive foreground is an instance of what James called the Indirect Approach to the objective situation through the trial-and-error of a Central Intelligence; but the Receptive Lucidity of a Strether, in *The Ambassadors*, is not at Marcher's command. Are we to conclude that the very nature of James' problem in "The Beast in the Jungle," the problem of dramatizing the insulated ego, of making active what in its essence is incapable of action, excluded the use of an active and searching intelligence in the main character?

The first of the two scenes appears in Part IV when years of waiting have driven May Bartram to something like desperation. She cannot overtly break the frame of their intercourse, which permits her only to affirm and reaffirm her loyalty to the role of asking nothing for herself; in the act of a new reaffirmation:

"No, no!" she repeated. "I'm with you—don't you
see?—still." And as to make it more vivid to him she
rose from her chair—a movement she seldom risked
in these days—and showed herself, all draped and
all soft, in her fairness and slimness. "I haven't for-
saken you."

We return to Marcher's mind, in which this reflection is all
that the moment can give him:

... He couldn't pity her for that; he could only take
her as she showed—as capable even yet of helping
him. It was as if, at the same time, her light might at
any instant go out; wherefore he must make the most
of it. . . . "Tell me if I shall consciously suffer."

Here we get a special case of James's Operative Irony, which
"implies and projects the possible other case." But the "possible other case" is not in the awareness of Marcher, as it always is in Strether; it is manipulated by James himself standing beside Marcher and moving May Bartram up close to
imply her virtual offer of herself, her very body—an offer of
which Marcher is not aware, so deeply concerned is he with his
"problem." As May Bartram stands before him, "all soft," it
is Marcher's Beast which has leaped at him from his jungle;
and he doesn't know it.

It is a fine scene, unobtrusively arrived at, and it has a certain power. It is perhaps sounder in its structure than the second and climactic scene. Marcher's frequent visits to Miss
Bartram's grave are occasions of a developing insight into his
loss, his failure to see that his supreme experience had been
there for him day after day through many years. But James
must have known that, to make the insight dramatically credible, it must reach the reader through a scene; and to have a
"scene" there must be at least two persons and an interchange
between them. He thus suddenly introduces, at the last mo-

ment, what he called in the Prefaces a *ficelle*, a character not in the action but brought in to elicit some essential quality from the involved characters. The stranger haunting the other grave is such a *ficelle;* but not having been "planted" earlier and disguised, he appears with the force of a shock, and could better be described as a *deus ex machina*—a device for ending an action by means of a force outside it; here it serves to render scenically, for the eye and ear, what had otherwise been a reported insight of Marcher's. James could not let himself merely tell us that Marcher had at last seen his tragic flaw; he must contrive to show him seeing it.

If this story is the greatest of the James *nouvelles*, as it probably is, one must reconsider the generally held belief that it is his special form, in which he scored greater triumphs than he ever did in the novels. If we look at it in terms of the visible material—the material *made* visible—it is much too long; the foreground is too elaborate, and the structure suffers from the disproportion of the Misplaced Middle (James' phrase). That is, he has not been able to render dramatically parts I and II and "confer on the false quantity the brave appearance of the true." If the grief-stricken stranger at the end was to be more than a palpable trick, should not James have planted him (or his equivalent) somewhere in the foreground?

These questions do not exhaust the story, which remains one of the great stories in the language. In the long run its effect is that of tone, even of lyric meditation; and it is closer to the method of Hawthorne than one may at a glance suppose; for in the last scene it is very nearly allegory, though less so than that companion piece, James' great failure in spite of its own great tone, "The Altar of the Dead." In neither of these stories is the naturalistic detail distinct enough to give the situation reality; and the symbolism tends to allegory because there is not enough detail to support it. We must always turn to Joyce's "The Dead" for the great modern example of the *nouvelle.*

III. The Dead

In "The Dead" James Joyce brings to the highest pitch of perfection in English the naturalism of Flaubert; it may be questioned whether his great predecessor and master was able so completely to lift the objective detail of his material up to the symbolic level, as Joyce does in this great story. If the art of naturalism consists mainly in making *active* those elements which had hitherto in fiction remained *inert*, that is, description and expository summary, the further push given the method by Joyce consists in manipulating what at first sight seems to be mere physical detail into dramatic symbolism. As Gabriel Conroy, the "hero" of "The Dead," enters the house of his aunts, he flicks snow from his galoshes with his scarf; by the time the story ends the snow has filled all the visible earth, and stands as the symbol of the revelation of Gabriel's inner life.

Joyce's method is that of the roving narrator; that is to say, the author suppresses himself but does not allow the hero to tell his own story, for the reason that "psychic distance" is necessary to the end in view. This end is the *sudden* revelation to Gabriel of his egoistic relation to his wife and, through that revelation, of his inadequate response to his entire experience. Thus Joyce must establish his central intelligence through Gabriel's eyes, but a little above and outside him at the same time, so that we shall know him at a given moment only through what he sees and feels in terms of that moment.

The story opens with the maid, Lily, who all day has been helping her mistresses, the Misses Morkan, Gabriel's aunts, prepare for their annual party. Here, as in the opening paragraph of Joyce's other masterpiece in *Dubliners*, "Araby," we open with a neutral or suspended point of view; just as Crane begins "The Open Boat" with: "None of them knew the color of the sky." Lily is "planted" because, when Gabriel arrives, he must enter the scene dramatically, and not merely be *reported* as entering; if his eye is to *see* the story, the eye must be established actively, and it is so established in the little incident with Lily. If he is to see the action for us, he must come authoritatively out of the scene, not throw himself at us. After he flicks the snow, he sounds his special note; it is a false note indicating his inadequate response to people and even his lack of respect for them. He refers patronizingly to Lily's personal life; when she cries out in protest, he makes it worse by offering her money. From that moment we know Gabriel Conroy, but we have not been *told* what he is: we have had him *rendered*.

In fact, from the beginning to the end of the story we are never told anything; we are shown everything. We are not told, for example, that the *milieu* of the story is the provincial, middle-class, "cultivated" society of Dublin at the turn of the century; we are not told that Gabriel represents its emotional sterility (as contrasted with the "peasant" richness of his wife Gretta), its complacency, its devotion to genteel culture, its sentimental evasion of "reality." All this we see dramatized; it is all made active. Nothing is given us from the externally omniscient point of view. At the moment Gabriel enters the house the eye shifts from Lily to Gabriel. It is necessary, of course, at this first appearance that *we* should see him. There is a brief description; but it is not Joyce's description: we see him as Lily sees him—or might see him if she had Joyce's superior command of the whole situation. This, in fact, is the method of "The Dead." From this point on we are never far from Gabriel's physical sight; we are constantly looking through his physical eyes at values and insights of which he is incapable. The significance of the *milieu*, the complacency of Gabriel's feeling for his wife, her romantic image of her lover Michael Furey, what Miss Ivors means in that particular society, would have been put before us, in the pre-James era in English fiction, as exposition and commentary through the direct intercession of the author; and it would have remained inert.

Take Miss Ivors: she is a flat character, she disappears the moment Joyce is through with her, when she has served his purpose. She is there to elicit from Gabriel a certain quality, his relation to his culture at the intellectual and social level; but she is not in herself a *necessary* character. It is to this sort of character, whose mechanical use must be given the look of reality, that James applied the term *ficelle.* She makes it possible for Joyce to charge with imaginative activity an important phase of Gabriel's life which he would otherwise have been compelled to give us as mere information. Note also that this particular *ficelle* is a woman: she stands for the rich and complex life of the Irish people out of which Gabriel's wife has come, and we are thus given a subtle dramatic presentation of a spiritual limitation which focuses symbolically, at the end of the story, upon his relation to his wife.

The examples of naturalistic detail which operate also at the symbolic level will sufficiently indicate to the reader the close texture of "The Dead." We should say, conversely, that the symbolism itself derives its validity from its being, in the first place, a visible and experienced moment in the consciousness of a character.

Take the incident when Gabriel looks into the mirror. It serves two purposes. First, we need to *see* Gabriel again and more closely than we saw him when he entered the house; we know him better morally and we must see him more clearly physically. At the same time, he looks into the mirror because he is not, and has never been, concerned with an objective situation; he is wrapped in himself. The mirror is an old and worn symbol of Narcissism, but here it is effective because its first impact is through the action; it is not laid on the action from the outside.

As the party breaks up, we see Gabriel downstairs; upstairs Mr. Bartell D'Arcy is singing (hoarsely, and against his will) "The Lass of Aughrim." Gabriel looks up the stairs:

> A woman was standing near the top of the first
> flight, in the shadow also. He could not see her face
> but he could see the terra-cotta and salmon-pink

panels of her skirt which the shadow made appear
black and white. It was his wife. . . . Gabriel was
surprised at her stillness. . . .

She is listening to the song. As she stands, one hand on the
bannister, listening, Gabriel has an access of romantic feeling. "*Distant Music* he would call the picture if he were a
painter." At this moment Gabriel's whole situation in life begins to be reversed, and because he will not until the end be
aware of the significance of the reversal, its impact upon the
reader from here on is an irony of increasing power. As he
feels drawn to his wife, he sees her romantically, with unconscious irony, as "Distant Music," little suspecting how distant
she is. He sees only the "lower" part of her figure; the "upper"
is involved with the song, the meaning of which, for her, we do
not yet know. The concealment of the "upper" and the visibil-
ity, to Gabriel, of the "lower," constitute a symbol, dramatically and naturalistically *active*, of Gabriel's relation to his
wife: he has never acknowledged her spirit, her identity as a
person; he knows only her body. And at the end, when he tries
to possess her physically, she reveals with crushing force her
full being, her own separate life, in the story of Michael Furey,
whose image has been brought back to her by the singing of
Mr. Bartell D'Arcy.

The image of Michael provides our third example. The incident is one of great technical difficulty, for no preparation, in
its own terms, was possible. How, we might ask ourselves, was
Joyce to convey to us (and to Gabriel) the reality of Gretta's
boy lover? Could he let Gretta say that a boy named Michael
Furey was in love with her, that he died young, that she had
never forgotten him because, it seemed to her, he must have
died for love of her? This would be mere statement, mere reporting. Let us see how Joyce does it.

"Someone you were in love with?" he asked ironically.

> "It was a young boy I used to know," she an-
> swered, "named Michael Furey. He used to sing that
> song, *The Lass of Aughrim*. He was very delicate."

Having established in the immediate dramatic context, in relation to Gabriel, her emotion for Michael, who had created for
her a complete and inviolable moment, she is able to proceed
to details which are living details because they have been
acted upon by her memory: his big, dark eyes; his job at the
gasworks; his death at seventeen. But these are not enough to
create space around him, not enough to present his image.

> "... I heard gravel thrown up against the window.
> The window was so wet I couldn't see, so I ran
> downstairs as I was and slipped out the back into
> the garden and there was the poor fellow at the end
> of the garden, shivering."

Up to this passage, we have been *told* about Michael: we now
begin to *see* him. And we see him in the following passage:

> "I implored of him to go home at once and told him
> he would get his death in the rain. But he said he did
> not want to live. I can see his eyes as well as well! He
> was standing at the end of the wall where there was
> a tree."

Without the wall and the tree to give him space he would not
exist; these details cut him loose from Gretta's story and present him in the round.

The overall symbol, the snow, which we first see as a scenic
detail on the toe of Gabriel's galoshes, gradually expands until
at the end it gathers up the entire action. The snow is the
story. It is not necessary to separate its development from the
dramatic structure or to point out in detail how at every
moment, including the splendid climax, it reaches us through

the eye as a naturalistic feature of the background. Its symbolic operation is of greater importance. At the beginning, the snow is the cold and even hostile force of nature, humanly indifferent, enclosing the warm conviviality of the Misses Morkan's party. But just as the human action in which Gabriel is involved develops in the pattern of the plot of Reversal, his situation at the end being the opposite of its beginning, so the snow reverses its meaning, in a kind of rhetorical dialectic: from naturalistic *coldness* it develops into a symbol of warmth, of expanded consciousness; it stands for Gabriel's escape from his own ego into the larger world of humanity, including "all the living and the dead."

Humanism and Naturalism

1929

I F THE NECESSITY for virtue could tell us how to practice it, we should be virtuous overnight. For the case of
the American humanists against modern culture is dam-
aging to the last degree. The truth of their indictment, nega-
tively considered, cannot be denied. But this is not enough.

There is a widespread belief that the doctrines of humanism are fundamentally sound. It would be truer to say that
they are only partly and superficially so, and that they are
being rejected for superficial reasons: the humanists are dogmatic, they ignore contemporary literature, they lack the
"aesthetic sense." These limitations go deeper. Humanism is
obscure in its sources; it is even more ambiguous as to the
kind of authority to which it appeals. And yet believers in
tradition, reason, and authority will approach the writings
of Messrs. Babbitt, More, and Foerster with more than an
open mind; they will have in advance the conviction that

> the rightful concern of man is his humanity, his
> world of value . . . that marks him off from a merely
> quantitative order;

but, after a great deal of patient reading, they will come away with that conviction—and with no more than that conviction. They will have got no specific ideas about values—that is to say, they will have gained no medium for acquiring them; and such a medium, they will hold, is morally identical with the values themselves. Values are not suspended in the air to be plucked. They will reflect, suspiciously, that the vague method of the humanist resembles the vague method of the so-called romantic in the very respect in which agreement or difference is fundamental: the humanist pursues humanism for its own sake—or, say, restraint for restraint's sake, or proportion for proportion's sake—and while this is doubtless better than pursuing disorder for disorder's sake, the authority of the worthier pursuit is no clearer than that of the baser. His doctrine of restraint does not look to *unity*, but to abstract and external *control*—not to a solution of the moral problem, but to an attempt to get the moral results of unity by main force, by a kind of moral fascism.

The reader will decide, moreover, that this defect of the humanist is a central one and that, critically examined, it will turn out to be the philosophical plight of the so-called naturalist. Doctrinal differences in themselves may be negligible; the man who supposes himself a naturalist may practice the humanistic virtues (Montaigne): the humanist in doctrine may exhibit the method of naturalism (More). But if the appearance of mere doctrine is deceptive, the use of a method cannot be. The humanists have no method. How, under the special compexities and distractions of the modern world, they intend to make good their values they do not say; they simply urge them. And this discrepancy between doctrine and method their hardier readers will find adequately described in Book II, Chapter IV, of the *Nicomachean Ethics:*

> ... yet people in general do not perform these actions, but taking refuge in talk they flatter themselves they are philosophizing, and that they will so

> be good men: acting in truth very like those sick
> people who listen to the doctor with great attention
> but do nothing that he tells them: just as these
> people cannot be well bodily under such a course of
> treatment, neither can those be mentally by such
> philosophizing.

The humanists have listened not only to one doctor but to
a great many doctors, and they tell us what they say; but
they have not learned, and they cannot teach us, how to take
the medicine.

I propose, in the first place, therefore, to analyze the position held by those humanists in whom the minimum of doctrine appears: I mean by the minimum of doctrine that their
thought refuses to exceed the moralistic plane: they steadily
repudiate all religious and philosophical support. The humanists of this type are Babbitt and Foerster. Secondly, I shall
try to discover how this humanism differs, if it does, from
that of Mr. More, who appears to lean heavily upon religious
values. If humanism shall save itself—that is to say, if it
shall find a method—what is the position into which it will
be logically driven?

I

The humanism formulated by Mr. Norman Foerster in the
last chapter of his *American Criticism* is actually a summary
of the views of Professor Babbitt. The summary is, of course,
an over-simplification, and does scant justice to Professor
Babbitt's intellectual resourcefulness; yet I think it contains
the fundamental scheme of his position. (It omits one of his
chief difficulties, which I will bring out in a moment.) The
assumptions of humanism, according to Mr. Foerster, are as
follows:

> (1) " . . . that assumptions are necessary." Foerster
> points out the self-deception of the naturalist, or the
> anti-authoritarian, who thinks he has got rid of
> assumptions.

(2) " ... that the essential elements of human experience are precisely those which appear to conflict with the reality explored by naturism. It [Humanism] recognizes, indeed, the service of naturism ... in showing the power of the natural man's impulses."

(3) " ... the central assumption of humanism is that of a dualism of man and nature ... the rightful concern of man is his humanity, his world of value and quality that marks him off from a merely quantitative natural order."

(4) "Finally, humanism assumes the freedom of the will to conform to a standard of values, as opposed to the deterministic assumption of naturism."

From these assumptions Mr. Foerster proceeds to a doctrine which I reproduce in a greatly abridged form:

(1) An adequate human standard calls for *completeness*. This includes "natural" human nature.

(2) But it also calls for *proportion*: it demands the harmony of the *parts with the whole*.

(3) The complete, proportionate standard may be said to consist of the *normally* or *typically human*.

(4) Although such an ethos has never existed, it has been approximately in the great ages of the past. Foerster looks mainly to Greece, but he includes the Romans, Vergil, and Horace; the Christians, Jesus, Paul, Augustine, others; the Orientals, Buddha, and Confucius; the moderns, Shakespeare, Milton, Goethe. (But he has misgivings about Shakespeare.)

(5) Unlike Romanticism, Humanism is true to its Hellenic origin in its faith in *reason*. It seeks to deal positively with the whole of human experience, in-

cluding those elements of experience that do *not* fall
within the scope of what it termed science.

(6) Unlike the conceptions of life that grow out of
science, Humanism seeks to press beyond reason by
the use of *intuition* or *imagination* . . . the human
or ethical imagination, as distinguished from the natural or pathetic imagination, which is below the
reason.

(7) The ultimate ethical principle is that of restraint
or control.

(8) This center to which Humanism refers everything . . . is the reality that gives rise to religion. But
pure Humanism is content to describe it *in physical
terms* . . . it hesitates to pass beyond its experimental knowledge to the dogmatic affirmations of
any of the great religions . . . it holds that *supernatural revelation must be tested by the intellect* . . .
it should be clear that Humanism, like Greek philosophy, *begins with science* and *not* with religion.

Now Mr. Foerster says that human values are those which
appear to conflict (do they or do they not?) with the reality
explored by naturism; and yet humanism demands the cul-
tivation of all human nature, including "natural" human
nature. He says, too, that humanism rejects the elements of
experience that fall within the "scope of what is termed
science." However this may be, humanism puts its faith in
reason (because of its Hellenic origin) and it is based upon
science, and yet it is unlike the conceptions of life that grow
out of science. It demands a dualism of man and nature opposed to the monistic assumption of naturism. But how, it
may be asked, is this dualism to be preserved along with that
other requirement of a "harmony of the parts with the *whole*"?
Mr. Foerster has just denounced the monistic whole. And,

further, it may be asked, upon which side of the duality does reason take its stand? If science is naturism, and reason science, the question answers itself.

Humanism is based upon science, which is naturism, and yet it is unlike the conceptions of life that grow out of science. Here it may be asked upon which science Mr. Foerster performs his miracle of accepting rejection? Is it just *science*? Or is it an unconscious attitude whose vision of reality is mechanism, a popular version of genuine science? In this case, it is the quantitative natural order of which he speaks. But how did it get quantified? Is it *naturally* quantified? The only plausible answer is that it was quantified by Mr. Foerster's kind of reason, but that being unaware of this he can, with an effective "chaser" handy, drink "reason" off neat.

The chaser is the "ethical imagination" which presses beyond reason. We have seen that he puts his faith in reason, and it is difficult to see why he wishes a faith beyond faith, or why he selects this particular super-faith: he refuses to press beyond reason in favor of religion.

His desire to go beyond reason is his desire to escape from naturalism. This conception of reason is contradictory. The mere desire to get out of jail will not unlock the gate, and you remain a prisoner: Mr. Foerster remains a naturalist. He says that "supernatural intuition" the phrase smacks of romantic Bergsonism—must be tested by the intellect. It is, thus, distinct from the intellect, not implicit in its action— a dichotomy that puts Mr. Foerster into the hands of the nineteenth-century Romantics whose evil he sets out to undo. This is the naturalistic, eighteenth-century "rationalistic" conception of imagination: irrational constructions of reality which "reason" (naturalism) may break down and reject. When Mr. Foerster says that religion and the imagination must be tested by the intellect, he therefore means tested by naturalism. For naturalism contains the only idea of reason that is available to the humanist.

If this were not true, the humanist would not be forced to

exceed reason. Mr. Foerster is a century behind the thought of his age: he is a romantic post-Kantian who can find no way out of mechanism but imaginative illusion. This imaginative illusion was the ethical imagination which Schiller found to be the only way out of scientism, and its origin is betrayed by Schiller's description of it as the ideal representation of causality. The difficulty for Mr. Foerster and Schiller is the question, How is this moral imagination to get itself moralized? You get nowhere by saying that the ethical imagination is above the reason, the pathetic imagination below; you have first to give them a motive for being what they are; without this you have a logical hypostasy, and the above and the below become "picture-thinking."

Mr. Foerster will have to decide to be scientifically reasonable, or not to be scientifically reasonable, whether he wants the parts to harmonize with the whole, or whether he rejects the whole for a dualism of the parts. He cannot have reason checking the natural and still keep it natural. Unless he can make up his mind, his dualism is merely verbal. He is expecting naturalism to unnaturalize itself—or, in other words, the imagination to make itself moral.

But perhaps after all he has a way out: there is one card remaining to be played, and it may turn out to be an ace. Now, the ultimate ethical principle is restraint or control, and the motivation of the ethical imagination is restraint; or at least it acts under the motive of restraint in order to achieve the "normally or typically human." This is the ideal towards which humanism strives, deriving its principles from ancient approximations of the ideal. But, if the ethical imagination is the instrument for creating the typically human, what it is motive for doing so? Is it restraint? Or is it restraining morality? Or is it restrained restraint? I hope I do not press this too far. You have got to go back to certain prior conditions under which an ethical imagination is possible. If the ethical imagination *is* imagination it must deal with images; but the humanists give us only a digest of the ancient cultures; they leave to abstract inference a conception of the particular culture in which the humane life may be lived. However wicked the personal life of Villon may have been, his imagination, under the conditions of his age, was bound to be ethical because it had a pervasive authority for being so; it could not escape this authority in some form.

It has been pointed out that Mr. Foerster's quantified nature has been quantified by his own kind of reason, and that he is, in fact, a naturalist. This brings us to one of the chief difficulties of Professor Babbitt's position.

Now Professor Babbitt, in order to escape from a passive Rousseauism, constantly opposes to it, notably in *Rousseau and Romanticism*, the ideal of the man of action, "who, as a result of his moral choices based on due deliberation, choices in which he is moved primarily by a regard for his own happiness, has quelled the unruly impulses of his lower nature." Again, in *Democracy and Leadership*, he writes: "To be completely moral one must be positive and critical."

This positive intellect, split off from the harmony of action possible to the unified, but not to the deliberately controlled, mind, is the very intellect that has supported naturalism throughout its history. It has created the self-seeking industrialist who *is moved primarily by a regard for his own happiness*. Professor Babbitt, of course, sees that this man *goes too far*; yet *how* far is *too* far? He has only the positive and critical intellect to tell him, and the best this can do is to set up an arbitrary limit to its own self-seeking activity— another instance of naturalism trying to unnaturalize itself. The stopping-place is pointed out by a study of the "wisdom of the ages," but it should be remembered that this wisdom must be discovered by the positive and critical intellect, which is supposed to use it against itself.

This, I believe, exposes the negative basis of Professor Babbitt's morality. The good man is he who "refrains from doing" what the "lower nature dictates," and he need do nothing positive. He merely refrains from complete action on the naturalistic level while remaining on that level.

It is clear that this is the source of Mr. Foerster's dilemma
—whether to suffer the slings and arrows of outrageous naturalism by "cultivating" it or to reject it altogether. Neither
Professor Babbitt nor Mr. Foerster conceives a unified "ethical imagination" moving harmoniously from the center outwards. They hypostatize it as a mediator, like Malebranche's
deity, an occasional visitor to the mind to be called in or
not, at will. The mind is a mechanical parallelism of moral
and natural forces arbitrarily distinct. The ethical force, being the mere negation of the natural, does not positively
oppose the supposed enemy because he is really his friend.
For this parallelism comes down to an attempt on the part
of the natural force to control itself by a law of its own
making—a law as various as the individualists who try to
formulate it.

Now the moralist in this predicament is not the Aristotelian
moralist—and I seem to remember that Professor Babbitt
aligns himself with the Stagirite. Professor Babbitt's moral
man deliberately undertakes to do, say, four good deeds a
day to *offset* his evil impulses, which thus are counterbalanced
but not transformed—just as the late Henry Clay Frick collected pictures to offset his transactions in steel. But the
Aristotelian deliberately undertakes the doing of "goods"
not at all, for to him there are no goods distinct from the
performance of his ordinary obligations, such as being polite
to his enemies or digging ditches, which become moral goods
only in so far as the man is a unified moral agent. His morality is not explicit but implicit in his specific moral acts,
which are moral or immoral according to his implicit moral
quality. Professor Babbitt's explicit morality is the finger of
the Dutch boy in the dyke, or the main sitting gingerly on the
keg of dynamite lest it explode. The modern problem is des-
perate, and Professor Babbitt recommends the police force.

From this position comes Babbitt's illuminating hierarchy
of social values. Men should be materially rewarded for three

kinds of labor, and in this order: (1) moral work, (2) intellectual work, and (3) manual work. The intellectual and the laborer are not doing moral work because they do not, while attending to their specific jobs, strive to propagate an explicit morality! Thus moral work is not qualitative but quantitative, and can be measured; it should be measurably rewarded. Doubtless it should; but meanwhile the honest laborer may be doing as much moral work as the professional moralist, and with considerably less self-righteous snobbery. Professor Babbitt's unshakable belief in the "war in the cave," interpreted through a categorical rather than a functional psychology, dooms us forever to a kind of Manichean illbreeding.

The conditions that should underlie the ethical imagination are by no means fulfilled by Mr. Foerster's doctrinaire summary of Sophocles, or of Vergil, or of Augustine, or his summary of these summaries, taken alone. You cannot get out of them a philosophy or a religion; for literature is no substitute for philosophy and religion. It is this vague understanding on the part of the humanists of the nature of philosophy· it is their lack of an exact logical and philosophical discipline, which betrays them, not only into the muddy reasoning that we have just seen; it leads them to expect to find in literature, ancient or modern, an explicit philosophy sufficient unto itself—a philosophy, in short, that does not already exist in some purer instead of a derived and literary form. They ask us, in effect, to burn the *Summa*, and to study Aquinas, as *Aquinas*, in Dante.

The belief held at various times since the Renaissance that the ancients are models of attitude and value is innocent enough; and it was useful so long as the classics could be assimilated to a living center of judgment and feeling. But, without this center, you get eclecticism—you get Professor Babbitt. And the sole defense of eclecticism is naturalistic— that is to say, it assumes the capacity of the mind to combine mechanically upon a *tabula rasa* a variety of unlike elements into a unity. We know that mechanical interaction, were it possible, could not yield a whole, but an aggregate. It expects Sophocles to fuse with Vergil without an agency of fusion. The humanist conception of literature is mechanical and naturalistic.

This is because its ingrained habit of mind is mechanical. The habit is the decisively important thing. The way one uses a method is, in the end, the doctrine, and not the literal significance of the doctrine's terms. The humanistic method, its ingrained habit of mind, is fundamentally opposed to its doctrine, and the sole condition under which this doctrine could be made good would be a center of life philosophically and morally consistent with it. Until this center is found, and not pieced together eclectically at the surface, humanism is an attempt to do mechanically—that is, naturalistically— what should be done morally.

Its idea of the "past"—of tradition—is infinite regression. When it is asked for "authority," it is constantly driven back from one position to another. We arrive at last at the "wisdom of the ages"—but can this wisdom by taken in and evaluated by a mind that has no way of knowing that it is wise? Professor Babbitt is a learned and distinguished man, and he may be wise. But for this we have only his word, since his morality, as we have seen, is only an arbitrarily individualistic *check upon itself*: his wisdom is a naturalistically historical recovery of the past.

The idea of infinite regression to authoritative judgment inheres in the thought of Foerster and Babbitt, and it is probably the subtlest fallacy to which humanism is committed. It takes all the *time* out of the past and all the concreteness out of the present. This fallacy is due to an unconscious transformation of the idea of an increasingly distant temporal past into the idea of a logical series which is quite timeless. This is another pitfall of picture-thinking: time is confused with logical succession, which, of course, may run in any "direction" or all directions at once. The humanist thus convinces himself that his logical series is a temporal past, and as such affords him a stopping-place—some fixed doctrine or some self-contained wisdom of the ages. But there can be no absolute in a logical series because all its terms are equal and it never ends.

Now the logical series is quantitative, the abstraction of space. The temporal series is, on the other hand, space concrete. Concrete, temporal experience implies the existence of a temporal past, and it is the foundation of the religious imagination; that is to say, the only way to think of the past independently of Mr. Foerster's naturalism is to think religiously; and conversely, the only way to think religiously is to think in time. Naturalistic science is timeless. A doctrine based upon it, whether explicitly or not, can have no past, no idea of tradition, no fixed center of life. The "typically human" is a term that cannot exist apart from some other term; it is not an absolute; it is fluid and unfixed.

To de-temporize the past is to reduce it to an abstract lump. To take from the present its concrete fullness is to refuse to let standards work from the inside. It follows that "decorum" must be "imposed" from above. Thus there are never specific moral problems (the subject matter of the arts) but only fixed general doctrines without subject matter— that is to say, without "nature."

The "historical method," says Mr. Foerster, rose in the age of naturalism, but he wishes to keep it as a valuable adjunct to humanism. It is a wish that humanism may rise upon its own debris, the miracle of naturalism unnaturalizing itself. Men cannot be naturalists with one half of the mind, humanists with the other; or does Mr. Foerster desire the growth of two cooperating classes—naturalists and humanists? The convictions of the one class are bound to undermine those of the other. The "historical method" has always been the anti-historical method. Its aim is to contemporize the past. Its real effect is to de-temporize it. The past becomes a causal series, and timeless; and as a quantitative abstraction (as Foerster himself sees) valueless. Are we to infer that, after the historical naturalists have done their work, the humanist will intercede and evaluate? This is the Victorian and naturalistic illusion all over again—that good may somehow be the "goal of ill."

Professor Babbitt has acutely charged the experimental moderns with not being experimental enough—they have not, he says, questioned the assumptions of their time, but swallowed them whole. He himself continues to experiment, but, as Mr. Eliot has pointed out, we cannot go on experimenting indefinitely. The reason why Professor Babbitt remains an inveterate experimenter is that he, in his turn, has not been philosophical enough. He constantly repudiates "aesthetics," which he believes to be a trivial decoration of moral doctrine; yet in literature the aesthetic approach is necessarily the philosophical approach. The dilemma between decoration externally imposed and imposed morality is false, and Professor Babbitt merely prefers the pot to the kettle.

The Socratic method, which he and Mr. Foerster after him apply so ably to contemporary society, is a method only, and it may be used by the humanist and his critic alike. Torn out of the Platonic dialogues, it is an instrument for the exposure of contradiction; it brings with it no motive for the exposure; it yields no absolutes. This will be made clearer in a brief analysis of the humanism of Paul Elmer More.

II

If Professor Babbitt's humanism is eclectic, Mr. More's is equally so—but the apparent synthesis takes place on the religious plane. Humanists like Babbitt and Foerster have to meet the problem of access to truth beyond the personality: it is obvious that Babbitt is a sound man, that his views are sound because he is; but there is no other guarantee of the soundness of his views. He is a "personality," and there is nothing to do about personality but to feel that it is sound or unsound. Mr. More, however, compels us to answer the question: Is his religion as a source of moral authority sound or unsound?

The problem is harder than that of personality, but in the end it is the same. What, in the first place, is Mr. More's religion? Is it Christianity? It is possible that it is. He has written time and again about the insight afforded us by Christian writers, and to them he has brought no inconsiderable insight of his own. There is also, according to Mr. More, a profound insight in Plato—perhaps the profoundest. Again, his studies in the Hindu religions and philosophies have stimulated him to some of his best and most sympathetic writing: the Hindus teach a deep religious dualism. Mr. More's *Studies of Religious Dualism* is a kind of breviary of the good he finds in half a dozen or more religious attitudes. The question remains: Which of these religions is Mr. More's? The answer to this, I believe, is: Mr. More's religion is Mr. More's.

Now one of Mr. More's critics has justly called the five volumes of *The Greek Tradition* an "original and profound work"; yet does its originality and profundity bear upon the question of religious authority—the sole question that I am putting to Mr. More's religious writings? However, Mr. More's defender indirectly attempts to answer this very question; he says: "*The Christ of the New Testament* [contains] an exact and unmistakable explanation of his [More's] acceptance of the historic Christian revelation." I have examined this explanation as well as Mr. More's other religious writings; yet what "acceptance" means is not clear, for his Christianity excludes belief in the miracles and the Virgin Birth. There is a detailed analysis yet to be made of his religious books; still I think that my conclusion will be found to be correct: The historic revelation that Mr. More has accepted is largely one of his own contrivance. It is revelation on his own terms— revelation as revealed by Mr. More. It is a reconstruction of the historical elements in a pattern satisfactory to the needs of "independent faith" (his phrase), the authority for which is to be found solely in his own books.

He has written a good deal on religion, but it is not easy
to put one's finger on his conception of it. Because of the
discrepancy between the individualism of his religion and the
dogmatism of his judgments his explicit statements on the
subject tend to be vague. And yet he does have definite ideas.
Their most significant expression is in incidental commentary.
About twenty years ago he took to task an interpreter of the
Forest Philosophers for trying:

> to convert into hard intellectualism what was at bot-
> tom a religious and thoroughly human experience.

Is intellectualism incompatible with religion? If the experience was thoroughly human, was it also religious? Mr.
More thinks that it was. If intellectualism has no place in
religion, where does it belong? Mr. More's reply to this is
undoubtedly Mr. Foerster's conception of reason: Reason is
the exclusive privilege of what the humanists call naturism.
Religion is an indefinite unutterable belief. Mr. More, as well
as Babbitt and Foerster, cannot get out of this notion of
reason. Now, if religion is not allowed to reason, what may
it do? Shall it be contented with visions? I think that Mr.
More would say no; but he could not rationally say it. Mr.
More repeats implicitly the dilemma of Babbit and Foerster
—and a dilemma is very different from a dualism. You have
on the one hand scientific naturalism; on the other, irrational
belief—the "illusion of a higher reality" that is only an illusion. It is the familiar doctrine of the *philosophe*, that the
religious or ethical imagination is an aberration of the intellect, of naturalism. Mr. More would say that the religious
and the human join in opposing the natural. But if the religious and the human combine in the present state of Mr.
More's religion, which is individualistic, he is opposing naturalism with opposition. You cannot overcome naturalism
with "illusion" or an individualistic faith; the illusion and the
individualism are properties of the thing to be overcome. In

spite of Mr. More's religious attitude, most of my criticism of Babbitt and Foerster applies to him.

Mr. More's dilemma is implicit throughout *Christ the Word*, and it becomes explicit in an essay entitled *An Absolute and an Authoritative Church* (*The Criterion*, July 1929). Harassed by the demon of the absolute, he tries to find religious authority apart from the Protestant claim of infallibility for the biblical texts, on the one hand, and on the other, from the Roman claim of absolute interpretation of these texts. The solution of the problem seems to lie in the Eastern and the Anglican Churches, which offer "the kind of revelation which neither in book nor in Church is absolute, but in both book and Church possesses a sufficient authority." The merit of any particular church is beside my point, but Mr. More's idea of authority is very much to it, and he fails to make it clear. He admits that his authority may bring "the reproach of uncertainty," and the reader must conclude that the uncertainty is rooted in his persistently independent faith. The essay is a summary of Mr. More's religious thought, and it is forthright and fearless; but it ends in vague appreciation of tradition tempered by individualism. The dilemma of absolutes remains untouched because Mr. More seems to lack the philosophical impulse to think himself out of it.

He gives us, in the first chapter of *Studies of Religious Dualism*, something of his religious history up to that time (1909). He had repudiated Calvinism. He was drifting, but suddenly he found a book that initiated him into the "mysteries of independent faith"the kind of faith, one observes, that the romantic, the naturist, the Rousseauist, has supported all along. Now just how much independence was necessary? Mr. More had to make his decision individualistically, and he had, like Professor Babbitt, no way of knowing when he came to more than a personal stop.

His critics have accused him of a defective "aesthetic sense"; he has seemed to be preoccupied with the content of literature; he has little to say of style, almost nothing, except what he says impatiently, of the craft of writing from the point of view of the writer. With Professor Babbitt, he never permits us to forget his conviction that the problems of craft are secondary and "aesthetic" and that, if the writer is virtuous, the writing will take care of itself. The reply to this is not that such confusion of thought is unworthy of Mr. More—which it is. It is not enough to oppose to it an equal confusion—that his is due to a lack of aesthetic perception. His failure to understand the significance of style is a failure to understand most of the literature that he has read. It is his intention to examine the "doctrine" of a given work in the light of his own. We have just seen that it is difficult to find out what Mr. More's doctrine is. With what is literature, then, to coincide? Mr. More entertains false hopes of literature; he expects it to be a philosophy and a religion because, in his state of "independent faith," he has neither a definite religion nor a definite philosophy prior to the book he happens to be reading.

In *The Demon of the Absolute* he remarks that he is not concerned at the moment with artistic means; only with "results." This distinction runs all through Mr. More's writings; he is not concerned with the letter of religion or of literature —the means through which it exists and is preserved, the religion or the literature itself. Religious results, separate from religious means, become—if they become anything— independent faith. Literary results, that is, the didactic paraphrase of a work of literature, challenge or support independent morality. In either case the full content of the literary or religious text is left behind. When Mr. More tells us that a writer has a sound moral attitude, he may be right, but there is no reason to believe that he may not be wrong. His judgments, for us, are thus neither right nor wrong: strictly speaking they are meaningless. He cannot cite his independent faith because he has no text outside himself; it is rationally inarticulate; there is no way to communicate it.

Nevertheless, Mr. More evidently supposes that he is conveying it; else he would not continue to write books. His reasons for this supposition not only command attention; they are of great interest in themselves. Mr. More is, among other things, a Platonist. What is a Platonist? Is he a man who believes what Plato believed? Or is he a man who uses the Socratic method for the exposure of contradiction? If he is the latter, to what end does he expose contradiction? Since Mr. More obviously believes things that Plato did not, he is, if he be a Platonist at all, one by virtue of his use of the Socratic method. But why does he use it? There is only one answer: for the support of independent faith.

And yet he constantly draws upon Plato for quotations and analogies (he has written a book on the subject); he has the air of delivering his opinions from quoted authority. But owing to the distracting influence of the other authorities—Christ, the Forest Philosophers—that compose his independent faith, it is difficult to ascertain just how authoritative, at a given moment, Plato is. The real authority at all times, of course, is Mr. More. I need hardly point out that Mr. More logically drives himself into the position of spiritual exile and, if he speak at all, of arrogance to which he has consigned the romantic enemy.

The belief in the authority of Plato when More is the actual authority explains the poor quality of his literary judgments. Moral judgments are never more irresponsible than when the judge supposes that the high and mighty of the past are behind him. Mr. More is a man whose critical habits are not subject to the purification and correction of specific objective standards, and the delusion that they are only increases their irresponsibility. In the name of restraint he is able to evoke the limit of his personal distastes.

Mr. More's fallacy is identical, as I have said, with that of the non-religious humanists. Because he cannot find an adequate conception of concrete tradition (experience) in terms of authority (reason), he gives us abstract, timeless, rootless, habitual ideas that closely resemble, in structure, the ration-

alism of the naturists. Authority in More becomes the spectral
sorites of infinite regress. There is no conception of religion
as preserved, organized experience; you have a mechanism
of moral ideas. Take this passage by Mr. More:

> True art is humanistic rather than naturalistic; and
> its gift of high and permanent pleasure is the re-
> sponse of our own breast to the artist's delicately
> revealed sense of that divine control moving like the
> spirit of God upon the face of the waters.

> So far I seem to see my way clear. If you should
> ask me by what rhetorical devices or by what instru-
> ment of representation one poem ... appeals more
> successfully than another to the higher faculty with-
> in us, how, for instance, Milton's *Paradise Lost* ac-
> complishes this end better than Blackmore's *King
> Arthur*, though *both poems were written with equal-
> ly good intentions* [italics mine]; I would reply
> frankly that the solution of this problem of the im-
> agination may be beyond my powers of critical
> analysis.

The first part of this passage is a fair example of the pulpit
rhetoric into which Mr. More plunges when he speaks of the
relation of literature to religion, and the reason why his
thought is vague is that, like Professor Babbitt, he has not
been philosophical enough; he has not examined his own
assumptions. It is difficult to distinguish, in the above quotation, any reason why true art is humanistic; for the "high
and permanent pleasure" and "the divine control" are only
pleasant ways of naming mechanical habits of thought. Mr.
More has never philosophized his ideas into ultimates—those
fixed yet interpretive, flexible positions from the viewpoint
of which the ghost of naturalism and the otherwise disem-
bodied spirit of morality become, not *things*, but experience
in the life of man.

As Mr. Eliot has pointed out in the case of Babbitt, More ignores the conditions out of which a book emerges. These conditions alone realize the author's ideas; they alone contribute morality, not an abstract, but a specific morality in terms of experience, to the work of literature. More cannot tell us why Milton is superior to Blackmore because his sole idea of the mind is that of a mechanism of moral ideas. The intentions of the two poems being equally good, he cannot understand why their equal morality does not moralize the pieces into an equal excellence; because moral ideas are *things* they ought to be as efficient in one place as in another. Mr. More conceives literature, first, as a mechanism of ideas; then, as a mechanism of books themselves; literature is a timeless, self-perpetuating machine set in motion in an infinite past which, being timeless, is not past at all. To be another Dante you have only to believe that his ideas, his "results," are good, and to identify them in some undefined sense with your own moral habits.

Mr. More's doctrine is morality for morality's sake, and if art for art's sake has always been an outrage upon reason, his position is no less so. Rationally there is little to choose between them.

His view of style as rhetorical devices is, then, perfectly consistent: the devices have no necessary connection with what is being said; like morality, they are superimposed. Morality being automatically moral, moral values are moral before they are communicated; the style merely dresses them up. But how can there be abstract results apart from the means—apart from the medium which, under concrete conditions, fixes the values in experience? Style—they way values are apprehended—is the technique for validating them. Mr. More's theory logically ends in never utering another word.

Because he cannot take the philosophical view he sees naturalism as the workship of instinct, license, self—all the things, in fact, that a respectable citizen of the United States for reasons of social habit would not permit himself to do.

This is admirable enough—but it is not philosophical. No one in his senses would deny that François Villon was a person of instinct, that he was pitiably engrossed in his own self, that he was a licentious fellow; no one in his senses would call François Villon a naturalist. The point as issue lies where humanism cannot take hold of it. The anti-naturalist is still a naturalist, if he cannot get off his naturalistic plane. Mr. More is a naturalist because he presents a mechanical view of experience. A doctrine is not a method, and until it can be made one, the humanistics are "flattering themselves they are philosophizing and that they will so be good men."

III

How shall we know when we have values?—a more difficult problem than the mere conviction that we need them. There is no such thing as pure value, nor are there values separate from the means of creating and preserving them. There are certain definite ways in which men have had access to value in the past (the humanists tell us that Dante had values, but not how he got them); but our problem is, Have we any of those ways now? If we have, how may they be used? Is there a condition or are there several conditions that must be met before we may use them?

We have seen the assumptions of the humanists. The assumptions of this essay are that humanism is not enough, and that if the values for which the humanist pleads are to be made rational, even intelligble, the background of an objective religion, a universal scheme of reference, is necessary. There should be a living center of action and judgment, such as we find in the great religions, which in turn grew out of this center. The act of "going into the Church" is not likely to supply the convert with it. Yet, for philosophical consistency, this is what the humanists should do. It is clear that this essay urges the claim of no special religion, and it is in no sense a confession of faith; but the connection between the Reformation and the rise of naturalism, and what I conceive the religious imagination to be, point to the position that the humanists must occupy if they wish to escape intellectual suicide. The religious unity of intellect and emotion, of reason and instinct, is the sole technique for the realization of values.

The virtue of religion is its successful representation of the problem of evil. The humanists recognize immoral conduct but they ignore evil in the religious sense. We have seen how Mr. Foerster, wishing at once to cultivate natural human nature and to reject it, could not decide how far he wished to go in either direction. This was because his dualism was verbal; there were no really opposed principles; there was simply an infinite number of points on the same scale. And thus his opposition between Quality and Quantity was verbal too; it was Quantity versus Quantity, presided over by rootless restraint, the referee who checked nothing but coherent thought. The humanists tell us that somehow we have to do with Quality, yet since for them nature is the qualified nature of scientism and the mind is a quantified machine of moral ideas, it is difficult to see where Quality comes from. The humanists seem to use the word to mean something "better" than something else—the philosophical level at which the fashionable tailor uses it.

There is, then, a preliminary question to be asked: What is the source of qualitative experience? Both horns of his dualism being reduced to Quantity, the humanist cannot tell us; and that is why much of his criticism gives us the feeling that he expects us to pluck values out of the air. Since the humanist has not been philosophically hardy enough to work out of the naturalistic version of nature, which he naively accept; since, in fact, he cannot root the concept of nature as Quantity out of his mind, his idea of Quality is irresponsible, foot-loose, highly transcendental in a kind of Concord sense.

The source of Quality is nature itself because it is the

source of experience. It is only by holding to an idea that leaves nature an open realm of Quality that experience is made possible at all; and, conversely, experience alone is the road to Quality. If a zoologist sees a certain Philippine corbra he doubtless says, *"Naja samaransis."* The snake is merely an instance of the quantification of nature. The head-hunter, however, has a more vivid feeling for the unique possibilities of the particular cobra; it may bite him; it may give him the evil eye—both richly qualitative experiences. For the humanist, *opposing* Quality to nature, has got it on the wrong side of his duality. Pure Quality would be pure evil, and it is only through the means of our recovery from a lasting immersion in it, it is only by maintaining the precarious balance upon the point of collapse into Quality, that any man survives his present hour: pure quality is pure disintegration. The scientist says, *"Naja samaransis"*; Mr. More, a cadence of the same theme—"Immoral"; Quality is quantified before we ever see it as Quality; and nature becomes a closed system of abstraction in which man is deprived of all experience whatever and, by being so deprived, reduced to an abstraction himself.

The religious attitude is the very sense (as the religious dogma is the definition) of the precarious balance of man upon the brink of pure Quality. But if you never have Quality, never have the challenge of evil, you have no religion—which is to say, you have no experience either. It is experience, immediate and traditional, fused—Quality and Quantity—which is the means of validating values.

Experience gives the focus to style, and style is the way anything is done. Rhetorical device is our abstract term for properties of style after style is achieved; they have never of themselves made one poem better than another.

Religion's respect for the power of nature lies in her contempt for knowledge of it; to quantify nature is ultimately to quantify ourselves. Religion is satisfied with the dogma that nature is evil, and that our recovery from it is mysterious ("grace"). For the abstraction of nature ends, as we have seen, with the destruction of the reality of time, and immediate experience being impossible, so do all ideas of tradition and inherited order become timeless and incoherent. It is the indispensable office of the religious imagination that it checks the abstracting tendency of the intellect in the presence of nature. Nature abstract becomes man abstract, and he is at last condemned to a permanent immersion in pure and evil Quality; he is forever condemned to it because he can no longer see it for what it is. He has no technique for dealing with evil. The protection of religion is the abstraction, not of nature, which so conceived would be the abstraction of abstraction, but of experience. It proposes a system of Quantity *against* nature; it is a quantitative version of the encounter between the head-hunter and the cobra. The organized meaning of the encounters of man and nature, which are temporal and concrete, is religious tradition, and though religious tradition is not exclusively the Church, it necessarily implies a way of life historically protected by the Church. The dogma acts for the recoil of the native from the snake: it is his technique for finding out the value of the encounter. Every such encounter is rich and unique in Quality: it is the temporal, never-recurring focus, the new triumph, the reaffirmation of the preserved experience of man. The modern humanist, because of habitual reactions, recoils, but he has no reason for doing so, and his recoil is without value. He and the cobra are one: Quantity versus Quantity; nature gainst nature; snake against snake; or, for that matter, man against man.

It is the failure of the humanist to get out of this dilemma which makes his literary criticism feeble and incomplete. Mr. Forester says: "It is best to face the issue in all candor"— the issue being Shakespeare. This poet merely "presents" life; he does not "interpret" it. If I had never read Shakespeare and had not read the rest of Mr. Foerster's book, his distinction would sound plausible; but having read his book,

I know what he means, which is something very different from what he thinks he means. He means that the mind of Shakespeare was not a mechanism of moral ideas. The humanists quarrel with literature because it cannot give them a philosophy and a church; but they keep turning to literature because they cannot find these things elsewhere. You cannot have the sense of literature without the prior, specific, and self-sufficient sense of something else. Without this you expect too much of literature; you expect of it a religion and a philosophy; and by expecting of it the wrong thing, you violate it, and in the end you get from it less than it is meant to yield; you get neither literature nor religion, nor anything that is intelligible. You destroy literature without constructing a religion.

For, as M. Ramon Fernandez has recently said, Humanism should not pretend to be a "body of Doctrine"; it is "a resultant situation."

The American humanists have tried to make the resultant situation its own background. Humanism is too ambitious, with insufficient preparation. (I do not mean erudition.) It tries to take a short cut to the resultant situation, and ignores the moral difficulty of imagining what the background should be; it is an effort to imitate by rote the natural product of culture; it is a mechanical formula for the recovery of civilization. It is the cart before the horse, and because it gets the "philosophy" in the wrong place, it invites philosophical attack. Humanism should be culture, but it may be a little untamed in the humanists until, as the digging of graves for the grave diggers, custom hath made it in them a property of easiness.

Translation or Imitation?

1970

L ADIES AND GENTLEMEN, I was delighted, honored, moved by the invitation to address this distinguished symposium.* The word "address" appeared in Mr. Basler's letter of invitation, and for a brief moment it filled me with dismay. An address is usually a formal oration proceeding through set Ciceronian tropes to a mighty peroration which sounds the trumpet of a prophecy. I am not sure that our foreign guests have heard the phrase "keynote address" or "keynote speech," so they will indulge me, I hope, if I explain this bit of Americana. A keynote speech is delivered at a political convention, Democratic or Republican, at which the party

---

*Poets from eight countries joined American translator-poets in an International Poetry Festival held at the Library of Congress April 13-15. 1970, under the auspices of the Gertrude Clarke Whittall Poetry and Literature Fund, and under the general chairmanship of the Consultant in Poetry, William Jay Smith. On Tuesday afternoon, April 14, Allen Tate addressed the symposium. Each foreign poet read selections of his works, and translations were read by the Americans. Foreign poets participating were, in order of appearance: Jorge Carrera Andrade, Ecuador; Nicanor Parra, Chile; Yehuda Amichai, Israel; Francis Ponge, France; Philippe Thoby-Marcelin. Haiti; Vasko Popa, Yugoslavia; Zulfikar Ghose, Pakistan; and Shuntaro Tanikawa, Japan. American translators in order of appearance were as follows: John Malcolm Brinnin, Miller Williams, William Jay Smith, Donald Finkel, Serge Gavronsky, and Harold P. Wright.

nominates its candidate for the presidency of the United States. The keynoter sets forth in ambiguous mixed metaphors the Utopian promises which neither the candidate nor other members of the party intend to keep or couldn't keep if they would. Now I cannot promise anything in this isolated, that is, isolated in midafternoon, keynote address. I cannot, for example, promise to survey, however briefly, the vast field of translations of literary works in this century. The arts of translating are now practiced throughout the world on a scale that could not have been imagined at the end of the nineteenth century. It is generally supposed that if the nations know one another's poetry, even if it comes through the translator's sieve, they will like one another better. This uncertain assumption, however, leads to something at once pleasant and quite certain. The poets themselves come to know one another, and this encourages in them the virtue of humility, for which poets are not notorious.

Never before in the Western nations has there been such an acute awareness of the literature of all nations, including those of the Orient and of Africa. Many nations outside the Western orbit are equally aware of us. Even an unpopular (or should I say nonpopular) writer like myself has enjoyed that remote attention through translations of some of my books into Arabic and Korean. (I wish I could read them.) To what extent this widespread reciprocal communication by means of translation is politically motivated one cannot at present determine, so great is our international political disorder. One might take the risk of a large generalization in a formula which would read somewhat as follows: the greater the political war of nerves the more resolved are men of letters throughout the world to create an international cultural medium. Or, at any rate, a medium that would be above politics or alongside the international struggle for power.

One is always a little suspicious of political poets, until one remembers that Dante's political motivation was an integral part of his divine vision. Of course, Dante would not have understood that curious word "motivation" which we use all the time. What is *your* motivation? What is *my* motivation? I think he would have said what is the *reason* for doing it. The value of such a poetry, in the end, an end that we cannot now foresee for our contemporaries, will depend on the talent of the poet, for a great poet can make poetry out of anything, even politics. Is it possible for us here at this conference to know whether there are great poets present? Each of us will have to answer that question in his own way or, more prudently, not answer it at all.

For many years I have had in mind what a seventeenth-century English poet, Abraham Cowley, said about the violence of the English Civil War as a milieu for poetry. He said it was a good age to write about later but a bad one to be writing in. Is our age like that, on a much larger and more formidable scale? I think it is. One's impression of our contemporary Russian poets is that of a daily struggle for the privilege of writing poetry at all. The hourly existential impact of a closed political system must necessarily make that impact itself the subject of the poem; or the poem would at least have to glance at it, or perhaps be a political counter-offensive against a hostile system. It is a situation that is not peculiar to Russia. Its permutations are visible in many other superficially different societies. W. B. Yeats' great political poems, "Easter 1916" and "1919," are tracts of the times and would remain only tracts were they translated literally into Polish or modern Greek or the language of any country which had suffered an abridgment of its liberties: a defeat to which the translator wished to show a parallel in the work of the Irish poet, but the translations would not necessarily be poetry, or certainly not poetry as good as Yeats' or even paraphrases which would have allowed Yeats to recognize in them a little of himself.

We do not know what poets behind the Iron Curtain or European poets this side of it think of us. Let us assume, which I don't with much conviction assume, that they envy us a little our rather wildly permissive society in which anything goes, even faked poetry, which on democratic principle we refrain from denouncing. For democratic principle forbids us to take a firm, critical line against poets who are merely "doing their thing." That's a great phrase in this country at the present time: *doing one's thing.* Now doing one's thing is every man's, every democratic man's, natural right, even if he doesn't know what a natural right is, and my thing is as good as anybody else's thing because it is mine. I trust you are not convinced that I believe our situation in the United States is as bad as the logical extremity that I have considered. I should, or I think I should, prefer our permissive society to the repressive society; and to that extent I participate unwillingly in the doctrine of doing one's thing, for I would rather do that than do somebody else's thing—for example, the thing that a government says I must do; and we must remind ourselves that all governments, even democratic governments, would like to tell us what to do, if we are not careful.

At the same time in our society we get a great deal of antipoetry, for we have poets who think that in order to be poets they need only to kill off the older poetry. Could we eventually have in America the destruction of all poetry as the alternative to a poetry which accepts some limitations proposed by society or by a church or by tradition? I take it that the history of poetry that we know anything about shows that a limitation of resistance has usually been good for poetry and that complete freedom may be as stultifying as censorship. We think of Dante as a poet who concentrated and defended the medieval order. The medieval order evidently did not want to be concentrated and defended by a poet, for the works of Dante were publicly burnt by Pope John XXII.

These observations seem to me an inevitable digression from the subject of our conference. The art of translation is our subject, or, more specifically, the application of this art culminating in a cultural exchange such as we are now enjoying. It is a commonplace of English and American literary history that translations from foreign literatures have had a decisive influence upon the re-creation of style. To go back no further than Milton, would *Paradise Lost* be quite what it is if Milton had not read John Sylvester's translation of an epic by a now-forgotten French poet, du Bartas? In our own time Pound's translations of Propertius had a powerful effect upon his original poems written later. It is irrelevant to say that certain scholars felt that Pound didn't know Latin very well. Would translations of Propertius by a great Latin scholar have been better? Better for whom? Certainly not for Pound. A pragmatic view of the art of translation is, it seems to me, the only useful view.

Let us imagine an impossible situation which may be applicable to us. Let us ask Propertius to come back and express an opinion of Pound's rendition of some of his poems. He might, could we teach him sufficient English, admire a passage here and reject a passage there, but he would not be capable of judging the literary merit of the translation. Were he capable of this judgment, were we capable of judging the translations of our poems, translators would not have to be called in. We could be our own translators. All that we are able to do, if we know fairly well the language into which our poems are translated, is to say that here the translation is not literal or it is simply wrong, or that on the whole it renders the intention we thought we had when we wrote the poem.

Now I hope that it will be no impropriety if I cite from my own experience an extreme and complex example of the use of translations. More than forty years ago I wrote a poem called "Death of Little Boys." This poem has enjoyed, or, if you will, suffered, a good deal of commentary. It has been held up as an example of obscure poetry. It has also been read as an elegy on the death of my own youth. Interpretations of a poem are further translations of that poem. The various interpretations of this poem constitute a fourth stage of translation from the original. The original is Rimbaud's *Les chercheuses de poux,* but I had not read Rimbaud's poem when I wrote my translation. I had read T. Sturge Moore's translation of Rimbaud. I was moved by the short scene in which some nuns are picking lice out of the hair of a lost little boy, a waif, who is perhaps nine or ten years old. Were this a seminar and not a lecture, I could become a professor and I would read all three versions for your illumination. By the time one gets to "Death of Little Boys," the Rimbaud original is so deeply buried as to be indiscernible. One of the commentators thought he had found my phrase "the cliff of Norway" in another poem by Rimbaud. I looked the poem up. I had not read it when I wrote my imitation.

The word "imitation" brings us to Robert Lowell's brilliant versions of poems beginning with a passage from Homer and coming down to the present with Eugenio Montale. Of the passage from Homer, which leads off in the volume entitled *Imitations*, one may say what Bentley said to Alexander Pope: "A pretty poem, Mr. Pope, but it is not Homer." This is true of Lowell, but it is irrelevant. What is wrong with Lowell's fragment of Homer is something quite different. It is not good Lowell. If I am right about this, then one would have to fall back upon a literal trot if no other translations were accessible, such as the prose facing the Greek in the Loeb Classical Library. It is more important to have good Lowell or good Pope or good Lang or good Chapman than a literal rendition, after we have gone beyond elementary Greek. Or, if we have no Greek, it is even more important to have a translation which is English poetry or French or German or Italian or Spanish or Russian poetry. For otherwise we mislead the reader without Greek into believing that Homer himself is mediocre. Had Thomas Rymer or Sir Richard Blackmore written a translation of Homer into which Keats had looked instead of first looking into Chapman's Homer, his own poetry might have been different, perhaps not so good as it turned out to be. I have been saying with some elaboration what we all know: that a translator ought to be a poet himself; that he must be a master of his own language, whatever mastery he may have of the language from which he is translating.

It has been recently said by several critics, and I have in mind George Steiner's essay on the subject, that we are now in an age of great translations. I think this is indisputable but, unlike literary criticism, which translations somewhat resemble, good translations are never obsolete. Literary criticism is perpetually obsolete. George Chapman's rhymed decasyllabic translation of the *Odyssey* is as good as it was in 1615, and I submit that Robert Fitzgerald's free blank-verse translation is as good as Chapman's. Do we need both? I think we do, but we did not know we needed Mr. Fitzgerald's version until we saw it. I shall not offer a list of great twentieth-century verse translations from various languages. I might just remind you of several, such as Lattimore's *Agamemnon* and Humphries' *Aeneid*. There is not enough time today to praise translations of modern poets, with one exception that I shall presently make, and there is no time, and this is not the occasion, for us to consider English translations of drama and prose fiction, which have on the whole been distinguished.

As I come towards the end of this discussion I would like to present an *exemplum*, a comparison of two distinguished but very different translations of the same nineteenth-century French poem. The poem is Baudelaire's but is not one of Baudelaire's great poems. It is the introduction of *Les fleurs du mal: Au lecteur*. The translations seem to me to be equally good, but good in different ways. But before I read them, I should like to digress into my own experience with Baudelaire forty-five years ago, if I can hope not to deceive myself about what I thought, as a young man, of Baudelaire. (There is nothing like the self-deception that literary men can practice on themselves after a number of years.) Men of my generation were led, and perhaps led by the nose, to Baudelaire by Arthur Symons, whose influence on modern American poetry, though indirect, was very great. Symons' Baudelaire was a poet of sin and vice, rather attractive sin and vice, and he failed to see that Baudelaire was the first great poet to respond to the horror of the overgrown, anonymous city. There was nothing in a late Victorian education, such as I had, and such as prevailed through the first World War, to prepare us to understand a poet like Baudelaire. More than Symons, the translations of a forgotten man named F. P. Sturm influenced a whole generation of young Americans. Looking back at some of my own translations, I am not sure whether they are direct translations of Baudelaire or parasitic versions of a little of Symons and a little of Sturm. That is always the risk that a young man runs who has not developed an idiom of his own. What he gives us is neither his own poem nor a poem moderately faithful to the original.

At what stage of his career is a poet qualified to translate the work of a foreign poet who is his peer? That is an unanswerable question, and here is another one: are we able to assume that a French poet and an Anglo-American poet who are contemporaries would do the best job on each other's work? This is not necessarily true. The two languages may not be contemporaneous, even though the poets are contemporaries. Longfellow and Tennyson could have made little of Baudelaire, and it is curious that Baudelaire thought Longfellow a first-rate poet. Swinburne made something of Baudelaire, but it is bad Baudelaire. It would be helpful if we could find a formula for the right relation of the translator to the translated. The two translations that I shall read seem to me to be masterly, though they will doubtless have to be done over again by a later generation. They may be the translations that we need. Do we need two very different translations of the same poem written at almost the same time? Evidently we do. I will now read the first, "To the Reader" or "Au lecteur":

> Ignorance, error, cupidity, and sin
> Possess our souls and exercise our flesh;
> Habitually we cultivate remorse
> As beggars entertain and nurse their lice.

Our sins are stubborn. Cowards when contrite
We overpay confession with our pains,
And when we're back again in human mire
Vile tears, we think, will wash away our stains.

Thrice-potent Satan in our cursed bed
Lulls us to sleep, our spirit overkissed,
Until the precious metal of our will
Is vaporized—that cunning alchemist!

Who but the Devil pulls our waking-strings!
Abominations lure us to their side;
Each day we take another step to hell,
Descending through the stench, unhorrified.

Like an exhausted rake who mouths and chews
The martyrized breast of an old withered whore
We steal, in passing, whatever joys we can,
Squeezing the driest orange all the more.

Packed in our brains incestuous as worms
Our demons celebrate in drunken gangs,
And when we breathe, that hallow rasp is Death
Sliding invisibly down into our lungs.

If the dull canvas of our wretched life
Is unembellished with such pretty ware
As knives or poison, pyromania, rape,
It is because our soul's too weak to dare!

But in this den of jackals, monkeys, curs,
Scorpions, buzzards, snakes—this paradise
Of filthy beasts that screech, howl, grovel, grunt—
In this menagerie of mankind's vice

There's one supremely hideous and impure!
Soft-spoken, not the type to cause a scene,
He'd willingly make rubble of the earth
And swallow up creation in a yawn.

> I mean Ennui! who in his hookah-dreams
> Produces hangmen and real tears together.
> How well you know this fastidious monster, reader,
> —Hypocrite reader, you—my double! my brother!

This version is by Stanley Kunitz. At a glance one sees that the stanza is the prevailing English quatrain frequently called the elegiac stanza, and in this Mr. Kunitz contrives an external assimilation of the poem to English usage. The original is in what we call in English the envelope quatrain, the most familiar example in English being the stanza of *In Memoriam.* Yet it is rare, and wherever used it calls attention to itself in English. I think that Mr. Kunitz did not want the reader to be distracted from what he makes Baudelaire say in English. I would like to call your attention to the phrase "what he *makes* Baudelaire say in English," for there is no English for precisely what Baudelaire says. We shall see in a moment that this poem is closer to the original than the other version that I shall presently read, but closer in the sense that Mr. Kunitz does not put his own individual style between us and our awareness that a poet had previously said something resembling what he, Mr. Kunitz, says. A simple example will illustrate the point. The first line of stanza two in the original is *nos péchés sont têtus, nos repentirs sont laches*: our sins are stubborn, our repentances are slack. It's pretty dull in English, isn't it? Mr. Kunitz runs the second half of the line over to the next line and attributes the slackness to the persons committing the sins. In short, what would be flat in literal rendition must be rendered dynamically in English. Now the second version is by Robert Lowell, and it is one of Mr. Lowell's best poems. Should a poem which purports to be a translation be better than the original? I hope that Mr. Lowell will forgive me the paradox: a translation should be as good, like Mr. Kunitz' version, but no better than the original. "Au lecteur" is not a mediocre poem (I don't think Baudelaire could write

a mediocre poem), but it is by the poet's own standards mere
verse—a versified statement of the argument of the entire content of *Les fleurs du mal.* The poem is not the direct and
powerful vision that one finds in one of the great poems like
"Les sept vieillards." It is expository, a catalogue of the sins
that man commits to relieve his boredom, for boredom is the
seat of original sin in this Gnostic view of man, Baudelaire's
gloss on the medieval doctrine of *Accidia.* Now let us see
what Mr. Lowell does with this catalogue of sins:

To the Reader

Infatuation, sadism, lust, avarice
possess our souls and drain the body's force;
we spoonfeed our adorable remorse,
like whores or beggars nourishing their lice.

Our sins are mulish, our confessions lies;
we play to the grandstand with our promises,
we pray for tears to wash our filthiness,
importantly pissing hogwash through our styes.

The devil, watching by our sickbeds, hissed
old smut and folk-songs to our soul, until
the soft and precious metal of our will
boiled off in vapor for this scientist.

Each day his flattery makes us eat a toad,
and each step forward is a step to hell,
unmoved, though previous corpses and their smell
asphyxiate our progress on this road.

Like the poor lush who cannot satisfy,
we try to force our sex with counterfeits,
die drooling on the deliquescent tits,
mouthing the rotten orange we suck dry.

Gangs of demons are boozing in our brain—
ranked, swarming, like a million warrior-ants,
they drown and choke the cistern of our wants;
each time we breathe, we tear our lungs with pain.

If poison, arson, sex, narcotics, knives
have not yet ruined us and stitched their quick,
loud patterns on the canvas of our lives,
it is because our souls are still too sick.

Among the vermin, jackals, panthers, lice,
gorillas and tarantulas that suck
and snatch and scratch and defecate and fuck
in the disorderly circus of our vice,

There's one more ugly and abortive birth.
It makes no gestures, never beats its breast,
yet it would murder for a moment's rest,
and willingly annihilate the earth.

It's BOREDOM. Tears have glued its eyes together.
You know it well, my Reader. This obscene
beast chain-smokes yawning for the guillotine—
you—hypocrite Reader—my double—my brother!

Mr. Lowell's version is dedicated to Mr. Kunitz; I wonder
if it was suggested by Mr. Kunitz'. Possibly, for it is obvious
that Mr. Lowell had two texts of the poem before him, Baudelaire's and Kunitz'. Lowell's penultimate stanza is closer to
Baudelaire's than that of Kunitz, but viewing the two versions
as wholes one feels that Kunitz retains more of Baudelaire.
Mr. Lowell is scrupulous in calling his version an imitation,
somewhat as Bach took over and amplified themes by Vivaldi.
Through the sheer violence of Mr. Lowell's rhetoric we get a
poem, which, by moving beyond the expository progression of
the original, achieves an intensity that Baudelaire neither in-

tended nor accomplished. We must be grateful for having two English poems where previously we had one French poem. The point I wish to emphasize is that the versatility of translation is without limit. In our time the arts of poetry cannot but profit by the cross-fertilization which has made the present symposium a necessary adjunct to the solitude of poetic composition. The Americans here today are indebted to our foreign colleagues for accepting our hospitality; and we fervently hope that at this moment of decline in civilized intercourse, we can preserve together, by creating anew, that order of intelligence without which mankind will not need to go to the moon. If we don't have that order of intelligence, we will have a sufficient desert right here.

III
EPILOGUE

A Sequence of Stanzas

Compiled and Read to a Group of Friends
on My Seventy-Fifth Birthday
1974

I. I strove with none for none was worth my strife;
Nature I loved and next to nature, art;
I warmed both hands before the fire of life;
It sinks, and I am ready to depart.

Thus, Walter Savage Landor on his seventy-fifth birthday:
a beautiful quatrain calculated to improve his "image" in the
eyes of posterity. If I am a member of his posterity, he succeeded until I learned a little about his life. Landor was a
frequent polemicist; he was, in fact, quarrelsome. At seventy-
five the fire of life sinks at least a little for everybody, but
Landor was not "ready to depart." He lived fourteen more
years. His heroic acceptance of death at seventy-five was
somewhat compromised. Should he have suppressed the quatrain, or perhaps rewritten it to conform to age eighty-nine?
My vague hope that I might adapt Landor's quatrain to my
life at seventy-five was quickly shattered. Some of it, the
philosophical part, I couldn't believe in when I was thirty-
two; or rather I believed that Landor's "nature," a benign
and responsive mother, had undergone, since 1850, a por-

tentous change: had changed, or been changed by man, from
the Latin *natura* (feminine noun), mother nature, into an
aggressive and destructive creature so vaguely human as to
cease being a *Thou* and to become an impersonal *It*. Here is
what I wrote in 1932:

II. Not, Landor, that I doubt your word
       That you had striven with none
     At seventy-five and had deferred
       To nature and art alone;
     It is rather that at thirty-two
       From us I see them part
     After they served, so sweetly, you;
       Yet nature has no heart.
     Brother and sister are estranged
       By his ambitious lies—
     For he his sister Helen much deranged,
       Outraged her and put coppers on her eyes.

Outraged her? In my boyhood it was a euphemism for
raped. Coppers on her eyes? Why? When I was a boy I heard
people say that the way to keep closed the eyes of the dead
was to put pennies on them. They must have been English
pennies; ours are too small to have sufficient weight. Putting
coppers on the eyes is a symbolic act, the final shutting off
the king of the senses. Beauty thus becomes blind and incapable of projecting herself upon nature, or may one say of
seeing herself in nature?

III. Ah, sad and strange as in dark summer dawns
      The earliest pipe of half-awakened birds
      To dying ears; when unto dying eyes
      The casement slowly grows a glimmering square.
      So sad, so strange, the days that are no more.

As one grows old the range of perception shrinks, so that
one hears not a lark or a mockingbird but an undifferentiated

pipe of half-awakened birds. Likewise one sees only a "glimmering square," not trees or hills through a window. A casement opens outwards *into space*, but here it opens on nothing but a glimmer. Is the person dying who sees this? Yes, and one must say, with this lyric as his authority, that we begin at birth to die. Whatever one's age, one's degree of consciousness shifts up and down. One saw trees yesterday morning, but this morning only a glimmer. If one here is dying, what is one doing in the last stanza? "Dear as remembered kisses after death."

After one's death one remembers in that next life the moment of love? Is one dead but still conscious of the deepest frustration that man can suffer? That is, hopeless love. I am stretching the meaning. But isn't it equally grim to face dead love in this life? "O, Death in Life!" We are still alive but at every moment something within us dies, until there is nothing left to die, and we are dead.

> IV.   In bulled Europa's morn
> We love our land because
> All night we raped her—torn,
>
> Blue grass and glade. Jackdaws,
> Buzzards and crows the land
> Love with prurient claws;
>
> So may I cunning my hand
> To clip the increment
> From the land or quicksand;
>
> For unto us God sent
> To gloze with iron bonds
> The dozing continent—
>
> The fallow graves, ponds
> Full of limp fish, tall
> Terrains, fields and fronds
> Through which we crawl, and call.

This passage of angry obscenity is from a poem of my own written many years ago in disgust with the behavior of Whitmanites like Carl Sandburg. It harks back to the ignorant Edenic *enthusiasm* of Michael Drayton in his "To the Virginian Voyage" and comes down to Sandburg's *To the People, Yes*. It struck me when I wrote the poem that the worlds of Whitman and Sandburg are inhabited, respectively, by two persons only: Whitman and Sandburg. So I don't know what people Sandburg was saying yes to or about. The men crawling in a blighted land could be post-ecological men, and may they be *us*? I don't like the gift of prophecy. But what can one do? When several poets have told so many egregious lies about one's history, one does the best one can —and this may be a vision of gnostic blight hovering at the threshold of consciousness—above or below it, waking or dreaming.

If nature has betrayed Landor's version of nature, we have destroyed nature. Nature does nothing to her-, him-, itself that we don't do. Nature is what we make her, him, it.

V.   For now the moon with friendless light carouses
     On hill and housetop, street and market-place;
     Men will plunge, mile after mile of men,
     To crush this lucent madness of the face;
     Go home and put their heads upon a pillow,
     Turn with whatever shift the darkness cleaves;
     Tuck in their eyes, and cover
     The flying dark with sleep like falling leaves.

When I wrote this poem more than forty years ago—and I quote here the second of two stanzas—I didn't like it as well as I now do. I was afraid of the last line. I feared that the "flying dark" might be more than a mere image for "falling asleep." I think it is more than that: it is flying into another world. But where *is* that other world—and *what* is it? The *where* is a stupid question, not unlike asking where the center of the cosmos is. What the other world is the next quotation tells us.

> **VI.**　The quarrel from the start,
> 　　　Long past and never past,
> 　　　The war of mind and heart,
> 　　　The great war and the small
> 　　　That tumbles the hovel down
> 　　　And topples town on town
> 　　　Come to one place at last:
> 　　　Love gathers all.

To say that the other world is love gathering us in has been said in different ways before, but never more perfectly than by Edwin Muir. This stanza has haunted me for many years. I am not sure that I know why I find it powerful. Every line is a platitude. But the eight lines are so put together, and so arranged rhythmically, that the result is brilliant and profound. Love is not mere love, whatever mere love may be; it is love gathering from the flying dark.

　Where do we go to be gathered? The question is inevitable, if stupid. When I met George Seferis in London in 1959 I could not have believed that later he would tell me how we must go. Here is our preparation for the voyage.

> **VII.**　All I want is to speak simply;
> 　　　For we have loaded even the song with so many
> 　　　　　kinds of music
> 　　　That gradually it sinks.
> 　　　And our art we so decorated that beneath the gilt
> 　　　Its face is eaten away.
> 　　　And it is now time for us to say the few words
> 　　　　　we have to say
> 　　　Because tomorrow our soul sets sail.

Acknowledgments

A Lost Traveller's Dream. *Michigan Quarterly Review*, Fall 1972.

The Fugitive, 1922-1925. *Princeton University Library Chronicle*, April 1942.

The Gaze Past, the Glance Present. *The Sewanee Review*, Autumn 1962.

Reflections on the Death of John Crowe Ransom. *The Sewanee Review*, Autumn 1974.

Miss Toklas' American Cake. *Prose*, Autumn 1971.

Memories of Miss Sylvia Beach. *Mercure de France*, August-September 1962.

John Peale Bishop. *The Collected Poems of John Peale Bishop*, edited by Allen Tate. Scribners, 1948.

Homage to St.-John Perse. *Poetry*, January 1950.

William Faulkner: 1897-1962. *New Statesman*, September 28, 1962; *The Sewanee Review*, Winter 1963.

Homage to T. S. Eliot. *The Sewanee Review*, Winter 1966. Also reprinted in *T. S. Eliot, the Man and His Work*, Delacorte Press, 1966.

Robert Frost as Metaphysical Poet. Lecture at the Library of Congress on the Centenary of Robert Frost's birth, May 26, 1974.

Introduction to *White Buildings* by Hart Crane. Liveright, 1926.

The Poetry of Edgar Allan Poe. *The Sewanee Review*, Spring 1968. Also appeared as introduction to *The Complete Poems and Selected Criticism of Edgar Allan Poe*, New American Library, 1968.

A Note on Paul Valéry. *Virginia Quarterly Review*, Summer 1970.

Shadow. *Carleton Miscellany*, Winter 1963.

Faulkner's *Sanctuary* and the Southern Myth. *Virginia Quarterly Review*, Spring 1968. Also appeared as introduction to *Sanctuary*, New American Library, 1968.

Three Commentaries. *The Sewanee Review*, Winter 1950; *The House of Fiction*, Scribners, 1951.

Humanism and Naturalism. *The Criterion*, July 1929; *Hound and Horn*, Winter 1930.

Translation or Imitation? The Library of Congress, 1970.

A Sequence of Stanzas. *Virginia Quarterly Review*, Spring 1975.

Index

Abercrombie, Lascelles, 97
Absalom, Absalom!, 83, 152
Adams, Léonie, 46-47, 48, 49, 54, 56
Agrarianism, 34, 42, 43
"Aim Was Song, The," 98
Album des Vers Anciens, 130
"Alone," 118-19, 120
"Altar of the Dead, The," 163
American Criticism, 172
American Notebooks, 159-60
American Library (Paris), 49, 55
"Anabase," 77
"Araby," 164
"Art and the Human Economy," 43
As I Lay Dying, 145
"At the Station," 36
Auden, W. H., 71

Babbitt, Irving, 170, 172, 177-82, 183
Back, Jacque, 28
Baker, Howard, 55

Barnes, Djuna, 57
Bartlett, John, 106
Baudelaire, Charles, 30, 111, 136, 201, 202-6
Beach, Sylvia, 51, 59, 67-68, 128
"Beast in the Jungle, The," 159-63
"Beyond Connecticut, Beyond the Sea," 70
"Birches," 103-04
Bird, William, 58
Bishop, John Peale: 69-75; death, 74; epitaph, 75; and Fitzgerald, 61, 62, 63, 71, 73; on Hemingway, 5, 60, 61, 73; and MacLeish, 72, 73, 74; and Tate, 55, 60, 61-62, 69; and Wilson, 71; writings, 61, 70, 72, 73
Bishop, Margaret, 61
Bogan, Fred, 11
Bogan, Dr. John Armistead, 14
Bogan, Louise, 109
Bogan, Samuel, 10-11

Bollingen Prize jury, 109
Bouts-rimés (parlor
    game), 54, 57
Bowen, Stella, 49
Boy's Will, A, 98
Bradley, William
    Aspenwall, 56, 58
Brooks, Cleanth, 44, 108
Buchan, Major Lewis, 9-10, 11
Burke, Kenneth, 69
Butt, Catherine Lewis, 8

Callaghan, Morley, 57, 63
Campbell, Killis, 119
Captain Singleton, 5, 60
Chestnut Hill, 8
Chills and Fever, 43
Church, Richard, 48, 97
"Cimetiere Marin, Le", 131,
    135, 136, 138-39
"City in the Sea, The," 122,
    125-26
"City of Sin, The," 125
Clarksville, Tennessee, 6
Clemens, Samuel L.
    See Twain, Mark
Cobbett, William, 5
"Conqueror Worm, The," 124
Cowley, Malcolm, 83, 119, 150
Crane, Hart: poetry, 110-14; and
    Tate, 30, 53, 57, 69
Criticism. *See* New Criticism,
    Poetry Criticism
Cullen, Countee, 48
Cummings, E. E., 32, 72
Curry, Walter Clyde, 26, 31

Davidson, Donald: 35-38; death,
    39; and the Fugitives, 24, 27,
    29; poems, 26, 35, 38;
    pseudonym, 29; and
    Ransom, 43

Davis, Jefferson: Tate's
    biography, 49-50, 55, 56
"Dead, The," 159, 164-69
"Death of Little Boys," 199-200
"Death of the Hired
    Man, The," 103
Defoe, Daniel, 5, 60, 145
Dendric (pseudonym), 29
Deus ex machina: defined, 163
"Discipline of Poetry, The," 73
Donne, John, 44
"Doomed City, The," 125
Double Dealer, The 30, 149
Dowson, Ernest, 126
Dunning, Ralph
    Cheever, 53-54, 55

"Ebauche d'un Serpent," 131,
    135, 136, 137-38
Eberhart, Richard, 109
Edel, Leon, 56
Eliot, T. S.: 44-45, 87-91, 126;
    Collected Poems, 42;
    on Pound, 36-37; and
    Ransom, 41-42, 44; and Tate,
    48, 88-89, 97, influence on
    Tate, 30, 87-91; on Valéry,
    132; *The Waste Land,* 30,
    111-12
"Emblems of Conduct," 112
"Empty Threat, An," 98
Essays of Four Decades, x
Eureka, 116-17, 124
Existentialism, 117-18
Expatriates, 46-66, 72-73
Expressionism: and formalism,
    140-41; and Poe, 124, 126

Fable, A, 84, 145
"Fall of the House of Usher,
    The," 155-58
Fathers, The, 9-10, 11

Faulkner, William: 82-86, 144-54; and Southern myth, 85-86, 151-52; and Tate, 82-83; works, 83-84, 145

Fauteuil XXXVIII, 51-52, 128

Fay, Bernard, 55-56

Feathertop, Henry (pseudonym), 29

Ficelle: defined, 163, 166

Finnegans Wake, 53

Fitzgerald, F. Scott: 48, 62-63; and Bishop, 61, 62, 71, 73; and Hemingway, 63; and Tate, 62-63, 66

Fitzgerald, Zelda, 48, 62

Flaubert, Gustave, 84, 149

Flecker, James Elroy, 77

Fleurs du mal, Les: Au lecteur, 201, 202-06

Flint, F. S., 48, 97

Foerster, Norman, 170, 172-82, 183, 193-94

Ford, Ford Madox: *The Good Soldier,* 58; and impressionist novel, 84; literary influences, 5; in Paris, 48, 53-55, 57, 58; and Gertrude Stein, 64-65; and Tate, 47, 48, 53-55, 57-58; and women, 49, 57, 60

Ford, Julie, 49

Formalists and expressionists, 140-41

Foster, Charles, 109

Fowlie, Wallace, 135

"Fragments de Mémoires d'un Poeme," 131

Frank, James, 24

French non-metrical poetry, 78-80

Frost, Robert, 95-109; poetry, 98-109; restricted diction, 105-06; and Tate, 97-98, 109

Fugitive, The, 27, 28, 29-30, 34, 42

Fugitives, 24-34; meetings, 24-48, 32; members, 25-26, 27, 31; pseudonyms, 29

"Futility: a Volume of Useless Verse," 26

Gallivant, Robin (pseudonym), 29

"Garden Abstract," 110

Georgia Scenes, 147

Gillespie, Lincoln, 53, 55

God Without Thunder, 41-42

Golden Mean, 32

Good Soldier, The, 58

Gordon, Caroline, 53, 60, 85

Great Gatsby, The, 63

Green, Julien, 51, 52

Guggenheim Fellowship, 47-48, 49, 96-97

"Hackberry Tree, The," 27

"Haunted Palace, The," 124

Hawthorne, Nathaniel, 159-60, 163

Hemingway, Ernest: and Bishop, 61, 62, 73; and the critics, 63; on Faulkner, 144; and Fitzgerald, 63; literary influences, 5, 60, 145; and MacLeish, 63; *A Moveable Feast,* ix, 54, 60; and Stein, 56, 64, 66; Sweeney, 50-51; and Tate, 54, 59-61, 63-64

Hirsch, Sidney Mttron, 25, 27-28, 29

"Hours, The," 73

House of the Seven Gables, 152

Howarth, Herbert, 96, 105

Huckleberry Finn, 147

Humanism, 170-94

"L'Idée Fixe," 132-33
I'll Take My Stand, 34, 42
Imagination: auditory, 106
Imagism, 110-11
Impressionist novel, 84
"In Amicitia," 45
"Introduction à la méthode de
    Léonard de Vinci," 129
Irony: classical, 159;
    operative (James), 162
Irving, Washington, 65
"I Will Sing You One, O," 98

Jackson, Thomas J.
    (Stonewall): biography, 49-50
Jacobs, W. W., 101, 102-3
James, Henry: 83, 86, 100, 101,
    161; "The Beast in the
    Jungle," 159-63; on the novel,
    84, 103, 155; Stein comments,
    65. *See Ficelle,* Irony
*Jefferson Davis: His Rise and
    Fall,* 49-50, 55, 56
"Jeune Parque, La," 136
Johnson, Samuel, 95, 105
Johnson, Stanley, 25
Jolas, Eugene, 53
Joyce, James, 149, 164-69

Kunitz, Stanley, 203-4, 206

Landor, Walter Savage, 122,
    211-12
Lanux, Pierre de, 62
Larbaud, Valéry, 51-52, 128
"Lee in the Mountains," 35
Leger, Alexis St. Leger.
    See Perse, St.-John
"Leçon de Valéry," 132
"Letter to Mr. B," 123
Léviathan, 52
Life of Cowley, 95
Light in August, 84, 145

Literary Review, 41
Litterature, 133-34
Little magazines: in the South,
    149. *See also* individual
    magazines
Longstreet, Augustus
    Baldwin, 147, 148
Long Street, The, 35-38
Lowell, Robert, 109, 200, 204-6
Lynen, John F., 99
Lytle, Andrew, 85

McDonald, Nancy, 53
MacLeish, Archibald: 74, 76, 77;
    and Bishop, 72, 73, 74; and
    Hemingway, 63
MacNeice, Louis, 71
Madame Bovary, 84
"Many Thousands Gone," 61,
    70, 72
Maritain, Jacques, 52
Markham, Edwin, 125
Marryat, Captain Frederick, 5,
    60, 145
Matthews, Jackson, 68, 135
"Michael," 106
Mims, Edwin, 28
Minute Particulars, 73
Mississippi writers, 149-50
Mr. Pope and Other Poems, 49
Mohrt, Michel, 145
Moll Flanders, 60
"Monkey's Paw, The," 102-3
Monnier, Adrienne, 52, 67
Monro, Harold, 48, 97
Moore, Merrill, 27, 29, 32
Morand, Paul, 52
More, Paul Elmer, 170, 172,
    182-90
Morley, Frank V., 48, 97
Moveable Feast, A, ix, 54, 60
Muir, Edwin, 215
Myth, 33, 36, 85, 86, 151

"Necrological," 26
"Neiges," 78, 80
New Criticism, 115-16. *See also* Ransom, John Crowe, and Winters, Yvor
Nightwood, 57
Now With His Love, 62

O'Brien, Justin, 135
"Ode to the Confederate Dead," 52
Odyssey: translations, 200-01
"Open Boat, The," 164

"Painted Head," 43
Perkins, Maxwell, 63
Perse, St.-John: 76-81; and MacLeish, 76; poems, 77, 78-80; and Tate, 50, 76; on Valéry, 79-80
Peter Simple, 5, 60
"Philosophy of Composition, The," 131
Pleasant Hill, 8-9, 10
"Pluies," 78, 80
Poe, Edgar Allan: 115-27; annihilation theme, 117, 120, 125; birthplace, 6; education, 121; *Eureka*, 116-17; influence on Hart Crane, 112; as literary journalist, 119, 123, 131; parents, 121; poetry, 118-19, 122-27, 132; prose tales, 116, 155-58; unity of effect, 155, 157
Poems About God, 42
Poetic diction: in modern poetry, 105-06
"Poetic Principle, The," 123
Poetry criticism: concept-emotion formula, 40, 41; form-content equation, 140-42; New Criticism, 115-16; structure-texture formula, 40; tension, 40-41. *See also* Eliot, T. S., Ransom, John Crowe, and Winters, Yvor
"Poetry and Painting," 73
Poetry Bookshop, 97
"Poets Without Laurels," 44-45
Pope, Alexander, 142
Porter, Katherine Anne, 85
Pound, Ezra, 30, 36-37, 49, 54, 72
"Prelude to an Evening," 43
Prim, Roger (pseudonym), 29
"Problems for the Modern Critic of Literature," 136-37

Quinn, Arthur Hobson, 121

Ransom, John Crowe: criticism, 40, 41, 44-45; Davidson, 43; death, 39; on Eliot, 41-42, 44; essays, 43-45; and the Fugitives, 24, 30, 42; poetry, 26, 42-43; pseudonym, 29; revision of poems, 39, 43; and the Southern Renaissance, 34; and Tate, 29, 34, 39-40, 41-42, 45, 90
"Rape of Lucrece, The," 16
"Rape of the Lock, The," 142
"Raven, The," 122, 126-27, 132
Read, Herbert, 48, 97
Religion and humanism, 182-94
"Revolution of the Word, The," 53
Riding, Laura, 25
Rimbaud, Arthur, 111, 113
"Road Not Taken, The," 105
Roberts, Elizabeth Madox, 150
Robson, W. W., 103
Romantic poets, 121-22, 156-57
Rougemont, Denis de, 52
Rural Rides, 5

Sanctuary, 83, 144, 145, 149, 152-54
Sandburg, Carl, 214
Seferis, George, 215
Sewanee Review, The, 82-83
Shakespeare, William, 44
Shakespeare & Company, 59, 67-68
"Shakespeare at Sonnets," 44
"Sleeper, The," 122, 125
Smiles, Samuel, 5
Song of Myself, 77-78
"Sorrows of Thomas Wolfe, The," 73
Sound and the Fury, The, 84, 144, 145, 149, 152
South, post-Civil War, 32-33, 35-38, 70, 145-48. *See also* Agrarianism, Myth, and Little magazines
Southern Renaissance, 32-33, 35-38, 71, 85, 145-50
Southern Review, The, 44, 149
Starr, Alfred, 26
Starr, Milton, 26
Stedman, Edmund Clarence, 125
Stein, Gertrude: on American literature, 65; and Ford, 64-65; and Hemingway, 56, 64, 66; her leisure reading, 55-56; salon, 47, 64, 65; and Tate, 47, 58-59; *Three Lives,* 56
Steiner, George, 200
Stevenson, Alec B., 25-26, 34
Stevenson, Burton E., 50
Stonewall Jackson: The Good Soldier, 49-50
"Stopping by Woods on a Snowy Evening," 107-9
Strong, L. A. G., 48
Sturm, F. P., 201
"Subject of Sea Change, A," 73
Sud, 62

Sweeney, Charles, 50-51, 62
Symons, Arthur, 30, 201

Tate, Allen: ancestors and relatives, 8-11, 12-14, 21-23; birth, 5-6, 7; bookworm as a child, 16-17, 18, 19; brothers, 6, 8, 15, 40; childhood, 7, 8-9, 12-13; Civil War biographies, 49-50, 55, 56, 59; daughter, 7; in England, 48, 96-97; essays, x; father, 7, 8, 19-21, 40; *The Fathers,* 9-10; Guggenheim Fellowship, 47-48, 49, 96-97; Kentucky homes, 6-8; literary influences, 5, 30; mother, 5, 6, 7, 8, 16-17, 18, 20-21; moving frequently as child, 7, 17; New York City years, 33-34, 47; in Paris, 44-66, 67-68, 128-29; poetry, 18, 31, 32, 49, 68, 90, 199, 212, 213-14; pseudonym, 29; schools, 16, 17, 19; *Sewanee Review,* 82-83; Southern Renaissance, 32-33, 35-38; summer vacations, 14-15; at University of Virginia, 52; Vanderbilt University, 15, 24, 30, 40; Washington, D.C. years, 10, 12-13; youth, 14-17, 19-20. *See also* Fugitives
Tate, Benjamin (brother), 6, 8, 40
Tate, Nancy (daughter), 7, 49
Tate, Varnell (brother), 6
"Tears, Idle Tears," 213
Tender Is the Night, 63
Tennyson, Alfred, 210
Tension, poetic, 40-41
Thackeray, William Makepeace, 100
Thomson, James, 5

Three Lives, 56
"To a Fetish," 27
"To Earthward," 98
"To Helen," 122-23
Toklas, Alice B., 55, 64
Tolman, Herbert Cushing, 41
To the People, Yes, 211
Tragedy: as action, 85, 137
Transition, 53
Translation, 195-207
Turn of the Screw, The, 100
Twain, Mark, 5, 147, 148

"Ulalume," 122, 123
Undertaker's Garland, The, 71
Undine, 18
University of the South, 51
University of Virginia, 52

Valéry, Paul: 52, 128-29; on
  Eliot, 132; essays, 129-30;
  method, 131, 135; on Perse,
  79-80; poetry, 130-31, 135-39
"Valley of the Dragon, The," 24
Vanderbilt University, 15, 24,
  30, 40. *See also* Fugitives
Vanity Fair, 71, 100
Varnell, Eleanor, 8
"Vents," 78-79, 80
"Voyages," 112

"Wanted: An Ontological
  Critic, 44
Warren, Robert Penn: and
  Bishop, 61-62; and Fitzgerald,
  63; *Southern Review,* 44; and
  Tate, 31, 48, 85
Waste Land, The, 30, 111-12
"Waste Lands," 41-42
Wells, H. G., 57
Welty, Eudora, 85
Wheelock, John Hall, 109
Wheen, A. W., 97
Whitman, Walt, 77-78, 112
Wild Palms, The, 83
"William Blake," 31
Wills, Jesse, 31
Wills, Ridley, 31-32
Wilson, Edmund, 52, 71, 119, 161
Winchester, Kentucky, 7
Winters, Yvor: 40, 41; on
  Valéry, 135, 136-37, 138
"Witch of Coös, The," 99-102
Wolfe, Thomas, 73, 85
"Wood-Pile, The," 107
Wordsworth, William, 106
"Work in Progress," 53

Yeats, William Butler, 88, 146,
  150, 197
Yoknapatawpha County, 84, 146
Young, Stark, 85